Foot Malpractice

Clark D. Miller, D.P.M.
Author

Eli Karp, D.P.M.
Editor

Ira Alan Grunther
Illustrator

M·F·P

Cover Design by: Tina M. Cipriani

© 1988 MFP

ISBN # 0-945019-00-9

Distributed by: E & F, Inc., P.O. Box 1945, Athens, Georgia 30603

TABLE OF CONTENTS

Chapters

Clark D. Miller, D.P.M.

Graduated from The California College of Podiatric Medicine in San Francisco in 1970.

Awarded a One Year Medical/Surgical Residency at The California Podiatry Hospital in San Francisco.

Dr. Miller is a renowned medical/podiatric expert for over 10 years.

Currently practicing Podiatric Medicine in Millburn, New Jersey which encompasses all problems of the foot, sports medicine, surgery, and bio-mechanical problems.

Dr. Miller currently resides in Millburn, New Jersey with his wife and three children.

DEDICATION

Francine, Gabriel, Mara and Alexis

ACKNOWLEDGMENTS

ACKNOWLEDGMENTS

Many people are responsible for helping me, at one time or another, in bringing this book to fruition. I want to thank my wife, Fran, and the children for their understanding and encouragement. I want to thank Ira Grunther for his wonderful illustrations and for how much they enhance this book. A special acknowledgment to my brother, Dr. Larry Miller for his teaching me the finer points of foot surgery and medicine. I acknowledge Dr. Eli Karp, my editor. His quest for excellence was always present while writing this book. A thank you must go to Dr. Timothy Field for his tremendous help in setting up the style and layout of the book. Last and not least I acknowledge my parents for making it all possible!

FOREWORD

FOREWORD

Our purpose in writing this book is to discuss malpractice involving foot care; and primarily the foot care rendered by podiatrists. There are, of course, other health care providers who treat the feet (these include orthopedists, internists, physical therapists, nurses, etc.), but our focus shall be on the care rendered by podiatrists, and specifically, the standard of care rendered by podiatrists when treating their patients.

At the time of the writing of this book there are approximately 9,500 podiatrists in practice throughout the United States. There are seven podiatric medical schools in the country.

While it is a relatively small profession in terms of numbers (compared to medicine with over 550,000 physicians), podiatrists have made and continue to make valuable contributions in the care of disabled and diseased Americans. The overall contribution and impact of this profession belies its relatively small number.

Despite the overall positive contribution which members of the profession make in caring for the foot ailments of many Americans, there are instances of negligence or malpractice.

This book will discuss what constitutes "malpractice." In the case of podiatry (which includes the disciplines of both podiatric medicine and surgery) the standard of "community care" refers to that care given throughout the United States.

The "podiatric community" is a relatively small one, and in some respects, because of schooling requirements and training, because of frequent interfacing between the

1

leaders of the profession and its practitioners (at conferences, seminars, through professional publications) there is general agreement within the profession regarding many of the standards of podiatric treatment.

This book will discuss some of these critical standards of care. We shall also look carefully at instances of malpractice, particularly in our case histories, which are illustrative of deviation from standard podiatric care.

What, then is malpractice?

Malpractice is a deviation from standard medical and surgical care as rendered in a given community. In the case of podiatry, as stated, that community is the entire United States.

Deviation from standard care, in conjunction with a bad result or outcome, constitutes **malpractice** or **negligence.**

Not all bad results are caused by **malpractice.** There are many more instances of so called **unfortunate medical results** (UMR) than there are of actual **malpractice.**

In this book we shall discuss the difference between UMR and actual malpractice.

In addition to examining actual instances of malpractice, we shall also examine the standard of podiatric care from which there was a deviation and which lead to an eventual malpractice.

Before discussing malpractice itself, however, we seek to give the educated reader of this book a very solid background about the fundamentals of anatomy (foot anatomy), and pathology (certain disease states very important in podiatry; notably; arthritis, diabetes, reflex dystrophy, infections). Other essential background material we cover includes the basics of laboratory medicine, sterile technique, and surgical principles. The book also includes a very valuable glossary of common podiatric terms and their meanings. Finally, there is a chapter dealing with illustrative malpractice cases.

It is not our purpose to make podiatrists out of our readers. For that they would have to first complete a minimum of two years of premedical science courses, and then enroll in a full time four year program in any one of the seven accredited colleges of podiatric medicine in the country. Also, there would then be the matter of completing either a one, two, or three year post graduate training program in any of the several podiatric medical subspecialties, including surgery, biomechanics, orthopedics, and others. It is a long, arduous road which the podiatric student undertakes when he commits himself to someday becoming a podiatrist.

Obviously, then, what we cover in the book, while necessarily broad in scope and at times somewhat generalized, may not cover what you the reader need to know about podiatric medicine and surgery. While the coverage is, of necessity, somewhat broad and generalized, the underlying principles and general standards of care are important.

Our purpose in writing this book is to provide the interested reader with a foundation about anatomy, pathology, sterile technique, office protocol (including obtaining informed consent) and from this to proceed to a number of illustrative cases of actual malpractice.

The cases will serve to demonstrate some of the principles we set forth and also to state what the standards are in the current practice of podiatric medicine.

INFORMED CONSENT

INFORMED CONSENT

Consent and informed consent, specifically, are very important in the practice of medicine today, and in any discussion dealing with the subject of malpractice.

A podiatric physician must obtain the patient's consent before any medical procedure is performed. The podiatrist who performs a procedure without the patient's consent may become a defendant in a battery charge.

Consent to treatment may be "express," that is, explicitly given both orally and in writing; or it may be "implied," that is, by the conduct or silent acquiescence of the patient, as for example, the patient who extends his arm for the physician to take a blood pressure reading or withdraw blood for examination.

The regular office visit to the podiatrist is another example of implied consent. As long as the visit is of a "routine" nature, there is no need for the patient to sign a special consent form.

The so called "emergency doctrine" of implied consent does not generally apply to podiatrists, unless there is a life-threatening situation and the patient is unable to give consent to life-saving emergency treatment. In this situation the law implies consent on the presumption that a reasonable patient would consent to life-saving emergency treatment.

The courts have ruled that a patient's mere consent to treatment is not sufficient, unless it is also "informed." By this is meant, that the podiatrist (podiatric physician) must inform the patient of such things as the proposed treatment, the material risks and benefits of the proposed treatment, risks and benefits of alternative methods of treatment, and the prognosis if no treatment is offered at all.

Informed consent requires documentation in the medical record. The use of an informed consent signed by the patient provides some evidence of consent, but should not be used as a substitute for a full discussion with the patient.

It is the responsibility, duty and obligation, and within the podiatric community standard, for a podiatrist to explain the proposed benefits, possible risks, and complications of any podiatric procedure which the podiatrist undertakes on the patient.

To avoid liability for lack of informed consent, the treating podiatrist should ensure that the patient has given a voluntary, knowledgeable (informed) consent to the proposed medical/surgical treatment. Generally, the following elements should be included in any informed consent document:

1. **A diagnosis of the patient's illness or injury:**

   In the course of the normal physician–patient interchange, a diagnosis (tentative or definitive) will normally have been given to the patient. It should be included in the informed consent to answer any eventual questions regarding the proposed treatment and its suitability for the problem at hand.

2. **Nature and purpose of the proposed treatment:**

   This should be explained in non-technical terms which the patient, as a layperson, can reasonably be expected to understand. Diagrams and illustrations may be used to explain anatomy and anatomical relationships as they pertain to the proposed treatment. The foot readily lends itself to such illustrations.

3. **Risks and consequences of the proposed treatment:**

Risks and consequences of any given treatment should be discussed with the patient prior to treatment. A consequence is something that can be expected to occur, for example, scar formation as a result of surgery and suturing. Postoperative pain is another consequence of surgery, generally expected and generally manageable. Postoperative infection is an example of risk or complication which might result from a procedure. All significant risks (such as infection) and consequences must be discussed with a patient prior to treatment and documented in the consent form.

4. **Chance of success; alternate methods of treatment; no treatment at all:**

Generally, most consent forms include:

1) The diagnosis.

2) Nature and purpose of proposed treatment.

3) Risks and consequences of proposed treatment.

Other elements which may be included are probability of success, which most podiatric physicians are loathe to put in writing, since a less than desired result may lead to a suit for breach of warranty for failure to produce the desired result. Still, while the doctor should try to foster a positive outlook in a patient prior to a treatment, he should also be careful not to mislead the patient or promise more than he knows he can deliver.

The podiatrist is obligated to disclose alternative methods of treatment with associated risks and benefits. This is generally done verbally, since it would not be applicable to discuss treatment plan B when asking the patient to sign an informed consent for plan A.

Finally, the podiatrist should also discuss with the patient the anticipated results of no treatment at all.

The items discussed under heading 4 are attendant to an informed consent. These items, however, should also be discussed with the patient prior to executing a consent form document.

Documentation of Consent:

Obviously, having a full executed, signed inform consent document will help answer the charge that the patient was not "informed" about the procedure and the possible risks and consequences.

Consent forms provide direct proof of the patient's express consent to a procedure and can help protect the podiatrist and other related staff against a patient's claim that consent was never given. However, the patient's signature alone on an informed consent document may not be enough.

The patient may attack the written consent form by claiming that he was nervous, the doctor used technical/-medical words which he did not understand; that he was given medication prior to signing the form which made him somewhat dizzy and disoriented; that he doesn't understand English, etc.

To protect himself against such claims, the podiatrist should fully document the consent discussion in the patient's medical records.

Whenever a patient is signing his consent form document this fact should be witnessed, and the document should be co-signed by the "witness," preferably a person who can be called upon some years in the future, if need be, to verify seeing the patient not only sign the document in question, but also to having witnessed the podiatrist fully explain the risks and benefits of the procedure involved. Most podiatrists will use a member of their office staff to witness the signing.

If the doctor has fully and adequately documented all the elements of an informed consent, any allegation of lack of informed consent will frequently amount to a test of credibility. The jury either believes the patient or the doctor. The medical records and informed consent document will make the difference.

For an informed consent to be effective as proof, it must include the elements of a valid consent form document, which should include at least three crucial elements:

1. A diagnosis of the patient's illness or injury.

2. A discussion on the nature and the purpose of the proposed treatment.

3. Risks and consequences of the proposed treatment.

Additionally, other elements which may be included in the informed consent include:

4. Probability of success using the proposed treatment.

5. Alternative methods of treatment, and their as-

sociated risks and benefits.

6. Risks, benefits, and prognosis if no treatment is given at all.

A podiatrist who discusses the above elements with his patient, documents the discussion in his medical records, has the patient or someone else legally authorized (in the case of a minor or incompetent) sign a witnessed consent form document should be well protected against unfounded claims of failure to obtain an informed consent.

SURGICAL TECHNIQUE – STERILE TECHNIQUE – STERILITY

SURGICAL TECHNIQUE – STERILE TECHNIQUE – STERILITY

Pre-Operative Considerations:

Elaborate precautions are taken in our day and age to protect the surgical patient from contamination. In this chapter we shall look at some of these precautions and list some of the considerations the surgeon must make prior to and during surgery.

The overall purpose of these precautions (gloves, gowns, sterilization of equipment, proper surgical techniques, etc.) is to eliminate as much as possible bacterial contamination of the surgically created wound.

A surgically induced infection is at best an inconvenience, at worst, it can be debilatating, possibly fatal. The reader should refer to the chapter on **Infections** to review the significance of such a complication.

The surgeon/doctor is well aware that every surgical wound is contaminated by at least a few bacteria, and that most of these organisms are pathogenic (i.e., disease causing). Contamination, leading to infection, can be created from a defect in the aseptic environment, which might include:

1. The scrubbed surgical team.

2. The patient.

3. The general operative environment, including the air in the operating room and the floor.

Aseptic and sterile are synonyms. Both terms refer to an environment which is free from living micro-

15

organisms capable of causing infection or disease.

The principles of sterile technique or asepsis are universally accepted by the medical profession, and apply to both the hospital and office setting. While podiatrists may perform a great deal of office-based surgery, they must still adhere to the same rigorous standards of sterile technique as their colleagues in the hospital operating room.

Let us consider the "surgical team," which usually consists of the "head surgeon," one or more assistant surgeons, a non-sterile (or non-scrubbed member), and possibly more members, depending upon the nature of the surgery.

The "surgical team" includes all those members who wear gloves, surgical masks, gowns, shoe covers, head covers, and related paraphernalia. The surgical team, with the exception of its nonscrubbed members, is considered "sterile," that is, free of micro-organisms which could infect the patient. Sterile technique, in its most fundamental sense, means that sterile may touch only sterile; and nonsterile may touch nonsterile -- the two may never mix.

Generally, if the scrubbed team functions as it should and observes the principle of sterile technique, it represents a relatively minor source of infective organisms to the patient.

There are elaborate rituals which the surgical team goes through, which make for great drama on TV and in the movies, and whose sole purpose is to adhere to the principle of "sterile technique." The principle of sterile technique is the reason for the hand-washing, the gowning, the gloves, the shoe covers, the head-pieces, the funny movements, the "do not touch me" message.

A more important contributor of bacteria to the surgical wound (and consequent surgical infection) is the patient himself. The sources from which patient borne bacteria emerge start with the skin. Skin cleaning of the patient should begin a day or two before the operation with povidone-iodine or hexachlorophene showers or baths (in the case of hospital surgery). In the case of office surgery, skin cleaning should be done shortly before the surgery.

The greatest source of contamination in the basically clean operation is the **operative environment**, a term that covers every other element in the operating room, from the nonscrubbed personnel to the air over the surgical wound.

Recently, technical improvements have been introduced in most hospital operating rooms to clean up the operating environment, particularly with systems such as the laminar flow ventilation systems. While this has been a valuable recent contribution to asepsis, much more important in the operating environment is the behavior of the "nonscrubbed," or "nonsterile personnel," and the proper sterilization and preparation of surgical equipment and supplies to be used on the patient.

It has been determined by numerous studies of operating room protocol that human activity accounts for most of the organisms in the air of an operating room. Movement or talking by the nonscrubbed staff leads directly or indirectly to the dissemination of the major portion of bacteria containing particles in the air. Members of the scrubbed team, so long as they are relatively motionless, contribute little to this contamination.

In the same way that there are definite steps in sterilizing surgical instruments or supplies, so too, there are rules of behavior or an "etiquette" in the operating room. The rules boil down to a "surgical conscience." By this is meant a realization that bacteria are ever present and pose a potential threat to the patient, that talking and excess movement are to be avoided; that sterile is to sterile; and nonsterile to nonsterile; finally, that any "break" in aspetic or sterile technique should be reported and corrected immediately. If necessary, in the case of a major break, the operation may have to be stopped.

Sterilizing Techniques: Autoclaving.

Sterilization is the complete elimination of microbial viability. The sterilization of surgical equipment and supplies play a major part in preventing surgical infection. In the autoclaving of instruments and operating room supplies, it is generally agreed that a 30 minute exposure to saturated steam at a pressure of 15 to 17 pounds per square inch and at a temperature of 250° to 254°F, provides dependable sterilization.

Each sterilization run must be carefully handled and the articles to be sterilized must be packaged properly and arranged in the autoclave in such a manner as to allow steam to reach them (otherwise they may not be "sterile" after the sterilization cycle).

Autoclaving must be conducted by responsible individuals who understand the principles involved. The surgical team depends on the personnel who perform this vital task to be responsible and conscientious in their duty, and they trust the articles they are to use on the patient are indeed sterile. If not, the chain of sterility will be broken, and the patient who is operated on with nonsterile instruments will likely suffer a serious if not fatal infection.

Supporting Natural Host Resistance To Bacterial Infection:

Intra-Operative Considerations For Sterility:

Research in the past few years has demonstrated the effectiveness of the body's immune mechanism in preventing bacterial invasion in the normal person. In addition to the operative considerations of O.R. protocol, sterilization, patient preparation, it is also essential that the surgeon and his O.R. team minimize injury to the tissue and preserve normal local physiology to support the body's natural ability to fight off bacteria (which are present, even in so-called "sterile" fields).

One such way to support the body's ability to fight off infection is by having the surgeon exercise meticulous surgical technique. The surgeon must avoid damaging tissue, his incisions need to be correct, his instrument selection and use must be correct, he must manipulate tissue properly, he should avoid rough or prolonged retraction.

The surgeon needs to select the correct suture material for closing. The sutures need to be used to approximate tissue accurately, without causing strangulation. The right number of sutures should be used, neither too many or too few.

Perhaps most importantly, the surgeon needs to have a fine knowledge of the anatomy of the area on which he performs his surgery. He must also know, ahead of time, the procedure he plans to perform, and alternate procedures, should any complication or difficulty arise from the original plan.

The above principles of surgical technique, if meticulously adhered to, will provide a surgical incision whose resistance to bacterial invasion will be at its best.

More Preoperative Procedures (Considerations):

Maximum control of infection requires maintenance of active host resistance, as bacteria cannot yet be totally eliminated from the operative environment.

Needless to say, the patient must be healthy enough to undergo the rigors of surgery. Since most foot surgery is "elective," that is, nonemergency, and which the patient freely and voluntarily "elects" to undergo, there is ample time to evaluate the patient preoperatively as to his state of health.

For example, a poor candidate for surgery, foot or otherwise, is a patient with low cardiac output and systemic hypoperfusion, since such a patient will have a seriously weakened local and systemic antibacterial mechanism.

A patient with a preexisting disease, such as diabetes, is a risk for any surgery. His diabetes must be controlled pre, intra and postoperatively, since hyperglycemia is known to inhibit leukocyte migration, and a low leukocyte migration means the body's normal host defense mechanism against bacteria is thereby compromised.

Any patient with poor or compromised circulation is likely to have poor wound perfusion and is at risk for infection. Such patients need to be evaluated very carefully preoperatively as to their suitability for surgery.

Normal intact tissue is usually resistant to bacterial infection. However, surgical and anesthetic procedures (both local and general anesthesia) cause aberration in host resistance. The physiologic **stress** of surgery means that a small contamination may be sufficient to overwhelm a weakened natural resistance.

Thus, it is essential that the surgeon/physician/podiatrist understand the basic principles of host resistance -- that is, mustering the patient's ability to fight off infection, to bolster the patient's resistance by new methods (such as antibiosis) and above all, by using already established practices of aseptic technique and meticulous surgery.

INFECTIONS OF THE FOOT

INFECTIONS OF THE FOOT

Disease entitles: cellulitis, septicemia, abscess, uicer, bacteremia.

Infection is a much feared word in the medical world. It is the body's attempt to fight off offending organisms. Infection can be thought of as part of the reparative process of the body when it has been injured.

While most infections are unpleasant and troublesome for both the patient and the doctor, they are oftentimes the unfortunate by- product of our modern day age of advanced technology and sophisticated surgery.

While modern day surgery has advanced to the point where the surgical environment is asceptic, there are still risks of bacterial infection, at all times.

Elaborate precautions are taken on the modern surgical service to protect the patient from contamination. These precautions range from chemotherapy to radiation, from steam sterilization to air filtration, and they even include the very architectural design of the operating room itself. These measures are the result of enormous effort, careful experimentation and accumulated clinical observations, and they provide the surgical patient today with an environment as bacteria-free as possible (See chapter on surgery for further discussion on sterilizing techniques, asceptic or sterile technique, and general surgical principles).

Clinical Manifestations Of Bacterial Infection
(General principles):

Bacterial infection of tissue usually presents clinically

either as **cellulitis** or **abscess**. **Cellulitis** is a spreading bacterial infection of the tissue planes, causing an intense inflammatory reaction.

An **abscess**, on the other hand, is a localized infection marked by a circumscribed area of necrotic tissue and pus. Bacterial invasion of the vascular spaces, with subsequent dissemination via the blood, is called **bacteremia** and is a life-threatening condition.

Septicemia denotes multiplication of bacteria within the bloodstream as a progression of bacteremia.

In **lymphangitis**, bacteria spread through the lymphatics. We shall now look a little more closely at each of these infective entities.

Ulcer, another form of inflammation, refers to a local defect of the skin (epithelial tissue, better stated).

Cellulitis

Cellulitis is a pattern of inflammatory reaction based upon location. The term designates spreading, diffuse inflammation of tissue often accompanied by suppuration. Unlike the **abscess, cellulitis** is poorly defined and tends to dissect widely through tissue spaces.

Although all bacterial infections that originate in tissues rather than in the bloodstream begin as cellulitis, most usually remain localized and form abscesses if not controlled.

Only certain bacterial species (streptococcus and some staphylococcus) usually spread through tissue as extending cellulitis.

The local manifestations of cellulitis are pain and local

tenderness, swelling, redness and local heat.

Rest is an important element in the treatment of cellulitis, for it reduces the possibility that muscle contracture will force the bacteria into lymphatics or veins. Cellulitis of the limbs can usually be aided by elevating the limbs. This procedure aids host resistance with abnormal blood supply and frees it of the impediment of dependent edema.

The bacterial organism most likely to produce the classic picture of cellulitis is the hemolytic streptococcus. Here, penicillin therapy is specific. For other bacterial species the choice of antibiotic is not clear-cut, and identification of the organism and its antibiotic sensitivity is required for effective therapy.

Abscess

An abscess is a localized collection of pus created by the accumulation of a suppurative exudate (pus producing discharge) within a tissue or a confined space. Abscesses are usually produced by the seeding of a tissue or a space by bacteria.

Abscesses may be deep or superficial. An example of a "deep abscess" is a brain abscess. Most abscesses of the foot are superficial. A superficial foot abscess can be detected by its localized nature, tendency to develop point tenderness and fluctuation on palpation.

All abscesses should be drained or excised, for they present a considerable hazard of further bacterial spread.

In all cases of abscess, the surrounding tissue demonstrates the characteristic features of an acute inflammation, which may, in the course of time, evolve into a chronic reaction. In the course of such chronicity, the inflammatory focus may be enclosed within a wall of proliferating fibroblasts and newly formed blood vessels, creating a barrier to the further spread of the infection. The surgeon refers to such a process as "walling off."

Surgical abscesses are most frequently produced by **Staphylococcus aureus**. Treatment may require antibiotic therapy in addition to drainage or excision, particularly if there are systemic signs of infection (fever, chills, malaise) or surrounding cellulitis. Staphylococcal strains are no longer commonly sensitive to penicillin, so a penicillinase resistant drug should be used even if such an infection has been acquired outside the hospital.

Fortunately most abscesses of the foot are easily recognized in the skin or subcutaneous tissue. The problem of **pointing**, or migrating, as may occur with deep-lying abscesses (of internal body organs, such as kidney or brain) does not arise often in the case of foot abscess.

The best treatment for an abscess is its removal, either by total excision (which may be a complicated, risky procedure in certain cases) or by incision and prolonged drainage with a drain kept free of coagulation by a wet and frequently changed dressing. Such a treatment also includes rest, elevation, proper antibiotics (based on sensitivity).

The best treatment, by far, is the prevention of infection in the first place by proper, sterile surgical procedures and postoperative care, the control of bacterial spread, pre and post operatively, at times with the judicious use of antibiotics before the operation.

Ulcer

An ulcer is a local excavation of the surface of an organ or tissue resulting from the sloughing of inflammatory necrotic tissue. An ulcer occurs when the inflammatory process is located at or near a surface. Ulcerative inflammation is most commonly encountered in two locations: in the gastrointestinal tract, and in the lower extremities in older individuals who have circulatory disturbances that predispose to skin lesions.

We shall briefly look at ulcers of the lower extremities. Ulcers may be of any size, and in the vulnerable individual may sometimes become spreading, ugly defects 10 cm. in diameter or greater. As stated, ulcers usually appear in individuals suffering from arterial disease (impaired blood supply to a region) or venous disease or both. Diabetes mellitus is another important predisposing condition to such ulcerative disease of the lower extremities (see Diabetes chapter).

Ulcer is mentioned briefly in this chapter because the reader should recognize that this disease entity is an example of an inflammatory reaction in the body based on location.

Lymphangitis

A bacterial infection of the lymphatic system (lymphangitis) or of the blood system (bacteremia) is usually caused by an extension of localized areas of cellulitis or abscess formation. Lymphangitis (or bacteremia) must always be immediately and vigorously treated with appropriate antibiotics. In addition, local therapy should be directed at the original lesion (such as an abscess) to include surgical drainage if necessary.

In acute lymphangitis there will be fever, chills, malaise, generalized aching and headache. Patchy areas of inflammation along the path of a lymphatic vessel resemble cellulitis. A lymphangitis occurring as a result of foot infection presents as irregular, pink, tender, linear streaks, extending up the limb toward the regional lymph nodes.

In chronic lymphangitis the lesion appears as a firm cord in or under the skin leading from the site of initial infection. The cord may be tender and may have abscesses, ulcers, areas of infection, or healed scars along its course where secondary foci have been established.

Lymphangitis is almost invariably followed by lymphadenitis (inflammation of one or more lymph nodes). Bacteremia (to be discussed) is a constant, life-threatening threat. Cellulitis with suppuration (pus formation), necrosis, and necrotizing ulcers may develop along the course of the involved lymph channel. The outlook in the case of lymphangitis for the very young, aged, or debiliated patient is often serious.

Bacteremia

We save the most serious of all infections (foot or otherwise) for last. **Bacteremia** refers to the presence of bacteria in the circulating blood.

Not all cases of bacteremia are fatal. But they are serious. There are different circumstances in which bacteria may be found in the blood stream. A transient bacteremia may occur following surgical manipulations (e.g., incision of an abscess).

Bacteremia is a common finding in systemic infections. There are quite a few signs and symptoms of bacteremia including: fever, variable in type, chills, skin eruptions, secondary infections.

Bacteremia is diagnosed by blood cultures, which should be for both aerobic and anaerobic organisms. Repeated cultures may be necessary.

As stated, bacteremia is a very serious infection. If the bacteremia is unresponsive to treatment or does not resolve by itself, the outcome is usually fatal.

Conclusion

As we have seen, there are different forms of infections which may begin in the foot (cellulitis, abscess, ulcer) and spread through the body (lymphangitis, lymphadenitis, bacteremia). The forms of infection we have taken up in this chapter include:

1. Cellulitis.

2. Abscess.

3. Ulcer.

4. Lymphangitis.

5. Bacteremia.

There are other forms of infection, although the five discussed in this chapter are the main ones. There are also several manifestations of infection, which can include inflammation at the site of infection and systemic manifestations, such as malaise, fever and chills. As we have seen, too, infection can spread from a local focus (as an abscess) along the lymphatics to the lymph nodes and into the bloodstream. Bacteria, viruses, rickettsias, parasites, and fungi can all cause local and disseminated infection.

Infections are serious, at times life threatening. If at all possible, they should be prevented, as by proper surgical technique. But once they occur, they should be treated promptly and vigorously to prevent further complications to the patient.

31

LABORATORY MEDICINE

LABORATORY MEDICINE

Podiatrists are trained during their professional schooling in the diagnosis and treatment of a wide range of ailments which may affect their patient.

Many systemic diseases are mirrored in the state of health (or ill health) of a patient's feet.

All podiatry college graduates must have taken and passed an internal medicine course, in addition to other related courses in diagnostics, laboratory medicine, histopathology, physical medicine, and more.

These essential courses are taught to the podiatrist in training to enable the doctor to assess a patient's general health status, to see the foot as an organ within an entire system, to appreciate and treat the patient as a complete, total human being who also happens to have a pair of feet.

The diagnosis and treatment of a patient, any patient, by any primary care physician (physician, osteopath, dentist, podiatrist) is derived from data that is collected and analyzed by a series of procedures.

Information is generally obtained by the doctor in three ways:

1. Information may be conveyed to the physician by the patient from the history of health or illness.

2. Information is obtained by physical examination of the patient. During this process the doctor will actually touch the patient, palpate joints, muscles, tendons, and use his physical senses to gather information about the patient.

3. Information may be obtained by laboratory or special examination (including radiographic study, which may be regarded as a form of laboratory study as well).

Obviously, the results of laboratory examination represent only a portion, albeit a very important portion of the information gathering process.

In medicine, laboratory results are often considered objective since reproducibility and accuracy are higher than the more subjective methods of physical examination.

Laboratory medicine plays an integral role in diagnostics. A podiatrist may routinely order a whole series of laboratory tests on a patient. A podiatrist, as the physician of the foot, is not required and in most states, is not allowed, by statute, to treat a patient's systemic disease (such as diabetes, heart failure, tuberculosis), but he would be expected to be alert to an underlying systemic pathology when evaluating any foot pathology, and standard podiatric care would dictate that he order the appropriate laboratory tests or make a referral to an internist or other specialist (such as a peripheral vascular surgeon or a rheumatologist).

As is true of much of medicine today, the field of laboratory medicine has undergone many changes in the past decade. Instrumentation and automation have permitted mass production of various tests and increased the availability of biochemical screening at economical rates and with improved quality control.

The individual practitioner in his small, private office (small, that is, compared to the facilities available in the average hospital) is limited with respect to the equipment (physical size and cost) and specialized operating skills required to carry on laboratory medicine.

Only relatively simple tests are usually performed in the individual practitioner's office.

While the podiatrist may choose to perform only a limited, small number of laboratory tests in his office, it is necessary that he be knowledgeable about most of the tests generally available in the field of laboratory medicine.

The laboratory tests we shall examine in this chapter are few in number, but crucial in the day to day practice of podiatry. Failure to perform some of these tests, the improper execution of any one of these laboratory tests, or the misinterpretation of of any one of these laboratory tests may mean the difference between standard podiatric medical care and malpractice.

The podiatrist must be ever mindful of his internal medicine if he is to avoid malpractice to himself and disaster for his patient. Consider, as an example, an all too often example, of the patient who presents to the podiatrist with an ulcer of his big toe. If this were a new patient, on his first visit to the office, the podiatrist would immediately suspect he is dealing with a diabetic or patient suffering from a peripheral vascular disease. As part of the medical workup of the patient, the podiatrist should at this time take a random, nonfasting blood test for glucose and a random urine test for sugar.

Fortunately, in this day and age, most patients who visit their podiatrist are under the care of a physician. The podiatrist would not be expected to treat a diabetic (if he does, he may be accused of practicing beyond the scope of his license), but he would be expected to be alert for this condition in any patient he treats, be able to order the necessary preliminary tests to rule out or confirm the presence of a systemic, medical condition, such as diabetes, and make a necessary referral for further medical management.

The community standards dictate that a podiatrist confer with other physicians about the medical condition of his patients, particularly when dealing with such chronic diseases as diabetes, gout, heart disease, hypertension, and arteriosclerosis.

A podiatrist who proceeds to treat an ulcer on the toe of a suspected diabetic, who is not under a doctor's care for his diabetes, may be rewarded with a malpractice suit for his foolish efforts.

Oftentimes, an unsuspecting patient may seek out the services of a podiatrist, thinking that his problem is strictly local and easily managed by the neighborhood podiatrist. Again, the podiatrist, because of his training, should be able to recognize when he is dealing with systemic conditions that require management by a physician.

At the initial encounter, the podiatrist may simply use his powers of observation to refer the patient to an appropriate specialist, or he may order a relatively simple test, such as a blood sugar or a urine test before proceeding with a treatment plan.

The field of laboratory medicine is vast, ever changing, complex, and unfortunately, with the advent of new, high level technology, rapidly becoming quite expensive.

When we speak of laboratory medicine, we include the areas of:

Clinical Chemistry (biochemistry).

Clinical Hematology.

Microbiology – Mycology.

Urinalysis.

Serology.

There are other specialized areas within laboratory medicine (such as virology, mycology, etc.) but the above 5 – ologies are generally thought of when laboratory medicine is mentioned. X– ray studies, ultra sound, and nuclear medicine are other adjuncts to diagnostics, but are not generally included in the field of laboratory medicine.

In this chapter we shall focus on certain tests which are of particular significance to the podiatrist in his everyday practice.

These tests include:

1. Blood sugar (glucose) – clinical chemistry.

2. Hemoglobin and hematocrit count – hematology.

3. Urinalysis.

4. Culture and Sensitivity – microbiology.

5. Fungal culture – microbiology/mycology.

Urinalysis

The analysis of urine, urinalysis, is one of the oldest and most basic laboratory study. Hippocrates, the father of medicine, is shown in lithographs examining the urine of his patients.

A standard urinalysis (as performed in most hospital and doctor offices) provides information about the following characteristics of urine:

1. Appearance.

2. Bile pigment.

3. pH.

4. Specific gravity.

5. Protein.

6. Sugar.

7. Ketone bodies.

8. Urine sediment.

The urinalysis is an integral part of the basic examination of patients in all branches of medicine. The particular aspect of the urinalysis which most concerns the podiatrist in his daily practice is the test for sugar. Fortunately, most of the enumerated elements of a urinalysis can be performed with a minimum of equipment and a minimum of expense.

Most diabetics perform an "at home" urinalysis to monitor the control of their disease by medication.

The podiatrist may perform a urinalysis as a screening device on certain patients, and possibly also on patients on whom he plans to perform surgery or other extensive podiatric procedures.

The "dip stick" method is best known. Most of the common reagent strips are plastic strips with reagent areas that change color in the presence of glucose or other so-called "reducing substances" in urine. The same principle used for the dip-stick test can now be applied to glucose testing of whole blood.

Glucose may appear in the urine of diabetics, particularly when their condition is not adequately controlled. A positive urine sugar test should alert the doctor to the possibility of diabetes, or some other medical problem. There are, however, other reducing substances which may give a positive dip-stick result, and these include sugars such as fructose, galactose, lactose, pentose.

When there is a positive urine sugar test result, other medical tests are indicated, specifically, blood sugar and a chemistry profile (the so called SMA series).

Diabetics, as stated, will frequently perform their own daily urinalysis, specifically the test for sugar, using one of the common commercial brands to monitor their insulin dosage and the management of their diabetes. A negative urine sugar (the desired result) indicates that the current dosage is probably the correct one. The information obtained by the dip-stick method may be useful clinically, especially in the regulation of patients with labile diabetes and in diabetes associated with a low renal threshold for glucose, as may occur in pregnancy. The dip-stick method gives a color reaction which is quantitative and can be compared with the color developed by solutions containing known concentrations of glucose.

There are other elements to the analysis of urine, including the quantitative examination of urinary sediment. Urinary sediment study involves the microscopic examination of the "formed elements" contained in urine:

Leukocytes.

Erythrocytes.

Epithelial cells.

Casts.

Crystals.

These formed elements within urine are generally indicative of some disease process within the body and would require further workup by the physician.

As a screening device and as a valid laboratory diagnostic test the sugar urine test is an integral part of the podiatrist's armamentarium for proper care. As such, the urinalysis, and specifically, the sugar urine test, should be performed when indicated if standard podiatric care is to be rendered.

During the glucose tolerance test, 50 to 100 grams of glucose, dissolved in water, is given orally in the fasting state and a determination of the amount of glucose in the blood (and the urine) is made before and at intervals of one-half, 1, 2, and often 3 hours.

Physicians evaluate and interpret the glucose tolerance test before making a diagnosis of diabetes, in most cases.

The podiatric physician/surgeon of the foot is very concerned about his diabetic patient. For one thing, he would carefully evaluate the risks inherent in any type of surgical procedure, or even a so-called routine or palliative procedure.

In the case of a known diabetic, the podiatrist would want to know if the disease is under control. He may test for this by ordering a urinalysis or a random blood sugar. In the case of a surgical candidate, he would also order these tests to rule out the presence of diabetes, and if diabetes is present, to be certain the disease is under control and that the patient's system will be able to bear the stress of surgery or other type of procedure.

The podiatrist's great fear for his diabetic patient is the possibility of infection. The patient with uncontrolled diabetes has an increased susceptibility to the acquisition and spread of infection, possibly because of the increased amount of sugar in the tissues, which makes a better culture media for bacteria. The mechanism may be unclear, but the possibility of infection in diabetics is always real and very threatening.

As we shall see in our case presentations, diabetics often have a compromised defense system. They are thus susceptible to infection of the foot (or any other body part). Infection may lead to gangrene. Gangrene, in turn, may lead to loss of limb, possibly even death. Often, a minor injury or insult to the body, such as may result from cutting toenails improperly, or paring a callus, inaugurates a process, aggravated by infection, and leading to devastation for the patient and doctor.

A relatively simple laboratory test, such as the test for blood sugar or urinalysis (sugar in the urine) may avert such disaster.

Hemoglobin/Hematocrit

Hemoglobin is the important element of red blood cells. It has physiologic significance in the transfer of oxygen from the lungs to the tissues and of CO_2 from the tissues to the lung. The podiatrist is very interested in knowing the hemoglobin and hematocrit values of his patient. These numbers can tell the podiatrist a great deal about the state of health of his patient and may provide some clue as to the patient's ability to recover from the stress of surgery.

The quantitative determination of the concentration of

hemoglobin in the peripheral blood is one of the most frequently performed laboratory procedures. It has importance as a screening test to yield a clue to disease that might not be suspected from the history or physical examination.

The concentration of hemoglobin is usually expressed as grams of hemoglobin per 100 ml. of whole blood. The so-called normal values may range from 13.8 to 17.2 gm/100 ml., depending on the method and instrument used. Expressed as grams of hemoglobin per 100 ml. of blood, the concentration of hemoglobin may vary widely in the blood of normal individuals. There are differences with age, sex and altitude. In the case of adults residing at sea- level, the normal range for males is 16 ± 2 gm/100 ml; for females, it is 14 ± 2 gm/100 ml.

Generally, a hemoglobin level below 12 gm/100 ml. may be considered to represent anemia. The physician would want to do further study on a patient he suspects of being anemic and he would be leery of performing surgery or other stressful, extensive work on a patient with a low hemoglobin count. A patient with a low hemoglobin count probably has compromised healing ability and is at risk of developing infection if subjected to the stress of surgery or other stressful procedure.

Hematocrit is the percentage of the volume of blood (sample) contributed by the red cells contained in that sample. Hematocrit is another hematologic parameter. Like the test for hemoglobin, and often in conjunction with it, it is a screening test for blood **dyscrasias** (disorders), and the general state of health of the patient.

The community standard of care in podiatric medicine /surgery would call for the podiatrist to determine the hemoglobin/hematocrit values of his patient prior to undertaking a surgery. A podiatrist who performs a surgery on his patient without obtaining these values preoperatively may be found to have acted negligently.

Fungal Culture

Fungal culture for the study of diseased, mycotic nails (fungus nails) employs any of a number of commercially available culture mediums. These mediums (which look like miniature test tubes) permit the simplified, rapid determination of fungi responsible for **tinea** infections of the skin, hair, nails.

Most often the test is based on a color change from yellow to red or a similar bright color. This color change is brought about by the growth of pathogenic dermatophytic fungi belonging to the genera **Microsporum, Trichophyton,** and **Epidermophyton.**

These are the three most common genera (pleural of genus) of fungus which commonly affect hair and nails.

The proper medical term for what the general public calls "fungus nails" is **dermatophytoses.**

Specific antifungal therapy for dermatophyte infection includes drugs such as **Griseofulvin** or **Tolnaftate.** Normally, after carefully trimming the nails ("debridement" is the term most commonly used by podiatrists for this procedure) the podiatrist will apply a topical liquid, such as lotromin solution or some commercial tincture directly onto the nails.

Any microbiological procedure, and a fungal culture of the nails falls within the scope of microbiology, requires a degree of skill and experience. Many of the commercially available test mediums obviate the need for sophisticated skills in microbiology in that they often require comparing a patient test tube color with a color print of the common genera.

Culture And Sensitivity (C & S)

Few physicians or podiatrists have the time, skill, or facilities for a complete microbiologic study. A culture and sensitivity is one laboratory test the physician most often sends out to a fully equipped laboratory. The physician or podiatrist, however, should be proficient in proper specimen collection, handling, and forwarding to a clinical laboratory facility.

Certainly, a C & S (as it is commonly referred to by health care workers) is a very crucial test which will be looked for in a patient's chart when infection has set in and complications arise in patient management.

One of the great fears for a podiatrist or any physician who performs surgery or other stressful procedure, is the onset of infection. Should infection set in, however, whatever the cause of the infection, podiatric community standards dictate that the doctor must be prepared to evaluate the patient's condition and proceed on a course of treatment. While an infection in any patient is always an unfortunate and undesirable complication of treatment, the responsible physician must be prepared to 1) evaluate the problem and 2) proceed with a proper course of treatment. Failure to do either is grounds for malpractice.

The culture and sensitivity test is the most commonly accepted method of determining the causative agent(s) of an infective process.

The **culture** part of the duo refers to the growth and identification of micro-organisms (generally, bacteria) on selective medium. The laboratory personnel will determine what media to use to grow the micro-organisms based on information given by the physician as to body site and clinical impressions. The **sensitivity** part of the test refers to the testing of the micro-organism, in a laboratory setting (in **vitro**) after it has been cultured, identified, and isolated to a series of antibiotics.

The microbiology laboratory, in addition to telling the doctor what micro-organisms are present at a body site can also tell the doctor which antibiotic, or series of antibiotics, would be most effective in combatting the micro-organisms.

While the physician may wish to proceed initially pending laboratory results on a course of antibiotic therapy based on his clinical judgment after years of treating similar infections, standard podiatric community care expects that he augment his treatment protocol with a laboratory result for culture and sensitivity.

Oftentimes a series of culture and sensitivity tests are ordered to confirm the causative agent (micro-organisms), best antibiotic, and response to treatment.

ARTHRITIS

ARTHRITIS

Arthritis refers to a whole host of disorders involving the musculoskeletal system. Most often when people speak of "arthritis" they refer to osteo-arthritis (also known as degenerative joint disease, D.J.D.).

Osteo-arthritis, the most common form of arthritis, is defined in the standard medical dictionary as a "non-inflammatory disease of joints characterized by deterioration and erosion of articular cartilage and by the formation of new bone at the articular margins, sometimes producing so-called spurs."

Osteo-arthritis is the most common form of arthritis. Other so-called arthritides include:

Reiter's syndrome.

Charcot's joint.

Rheumatoid arthritis.

Chondrocalcinosis (pseudogout).

These conditions are mentioned only in passing. The reader should always keep in mind that **arthritis** includes a host of maladies, with osteo-arthritis being the most common and the one most identified by the general public.

It is estimated that arthritis (osteo-arthritis) afflicts about 40 million Americans. Fortunately, only a small fraction of this number are significantly incapacitated.

Osteo-arthritis has been said to be as inevitable a concomitant of aging as graying of the hair. Those who advocate a vigorous, health conscious life-style dispute any such inevitability and attribute osteo-arthritis to an "improper" or unbalanaced life-style.

Aging is the single most important factor in the development of arthritis. (From now on, unless otherwise specified, when we speak of arthritis, the reference is to osteo-arthritis, or degenerative joint disease, as it is also called).

Virtually all persons over the age of 50 have at least traces of this condition. Another important factor which may contribute to the development of arthritis is medical or surgical intervention.

It is quite possible that the trauma of surgery may lead to the type of degenerative changes seen in other forms of arthritis. Such "doctor caused" (**iatrogenic**) arthritis may well be the basis of a malpractice suit. (See section on Surgery for poor results leading to arthritic joints). (See cases).

Other influences (besides age) contribute to the pathogenesis (i.e., natural progression) of this disease, although they are still poorly understood. **Osteo-arthritis** tends to appear earlier and to be more severe in patients with diabetes and other metabolic disorders. There are some indications of a familial tendency, but well defined genetic factors have not been identified.

Morphology - Characteristics of Arthritis

There are certain physical characteristics of osteo-arthritis which need to be understood, particularly when x-rays are discussed or when body parts are exposed for examination or during surgery.

1. Osteo-arthritis may occur as a uni-articular or poly-articular involvement. This means one or more major (and minor) joints of the body are

involved, for example, the hip joint, the knee joint, and in cases of greatest interest to us, the bunion joint (more accurately referred to as the metatarsophalangeal joint).

2. The large joints of the body including the spine are principally affected. Large joints of the feet, especially the first metarsophalangeal joint (bunion joint, so-called) may also be affected.

3. The principal anatomic alterations are degeneration of the cartilage, rather than inflammation of the synovia. With the destruction of the articular cartilage, the underlying bone is exposed. At the same time that degeneration is occurring, nature is trying to rebuild. Thus, small islands of cartilage may begin projecting above the surface of the articular cartilage, usually around the margins, to produce the characteristic **bony spurs** of osteoarthritis. These spurs are often responsible for the pain and limitation of motion seen in more advanced, painful forms of arthritis. Sometimes these spurs may fuse to form a solid, calcified bridge, thereby destroying all joint motion.

4. A further complication of the degenerative process may include fragmentation of cartilage or calcific spurs to form free intra-articular foreign bodies known as **joint mice**. When this happens, the capsule and ligaments of the joint often undergo calcification to further limit mobility.

Signs And Symptoms Of Osteo-Arthritis

Now that we have some understanding of the changes which occur on the cellular level when arthritis sets in, let us look at some of the clinical signs and symptoms of the typical arthritis patient as he presents himself in

53

the doctor's examinating room:

1. The onset of the disease is usually gradual and localized to one or a few joints.

2. The patient most often complains of pain and stiffness with little obvious disability.

3. Common symptoms include numbness and stiffness with pain on arising and after prolonged rest. The patient is otherwise well in most cases of O.A. (not so in cases of rheumatoid arthritis, R.A.).

4. The range of motion (R.O.M.) in the affected regions (joints) is usually limited, and extreme range of motion causes pain.

5. Tenderness and crepitus (a grating sound) are present over the affected joints.

6. The painful joints may or may not be enlarged and inflammed.

7. As the disease progresses, there is a gradual, firm, irregular enlargement of the joint. On occasion, the soft tissues are thickened as well.

8. Deformities, called **subluxations,** usually occur after many years of arthritis.

9. The characteristic enlargements of the interphalangeal joints (Heberden's nodes) may be found. **Heberden's nodes,** are found more frequently in women than men. These small nodes develop as bony outgrowths from the margins of the phalanges of the fingers. **Heberden's nodes** do not have to be present for O.A. to exist. Furthermore the existence of Heberden's nodes does

not mean the O.A. will become debilitating or severe.

10. In most cases of O.A., the disability is not as great as in R.A.. However, pain and swelling in different regions may develop (bony margins). Spurs may develop at the points of muscular, fascial, and ligamentous attachment, and go on to cause local irritation and disability.

11. Arthritis by itself is not bad. It is usually the added stress of weight bearing which aggravates the situation. This is one reason that arthritic feet are so painful.

Laboratory Findings/Other Tests/X–Rays

There is no definitive laboratory test to diagnose O.A. Usually the diagnosis is made based on the patient's history and the clinical examination. One very useful test, however, which may help in the diagnosis is the E.S.R. (erythrocyte sedimentation rate).

In severe cases of O.A., the E.S.R. may be slightly accelerated. Rheumatoid factor studies will be negative. Rheumatoid arthritis (R.A.) is the other arthritic condition which needs to be differentiated from O.A. in many cases.

Synovial fluid analysis is usually not helpful in diagnosing for O.A.

X–Rays: Radiographic Evaluation In O.A./Arthritis

Arthritis changes may involve the articular ligaments, periarticular structures, articular cartilage and/or synovia. There are, thus quite a few structures involved in arthritis, not merely the "joints." To understand radiographic changes noted in arthritis, it is necessary to have a little background on basic histology/anatomy of bones and joints.

Joints are made up by articulating ends of bone. These ends are covered by **hyaline cartilage**, not seen on regular x-ray. Radiologists often speak of the "joint space" which is really a misnomer. There is no "space," but, rather, an area of increased radiolucency. This means the x-rays penetrate the area and show a lucent (light) region when developed on film. In fact, there is articular cartilage in this area. A cartilage line (joint space) is uniform in width and the articular surfaces of the bones are smooth and have rounded margins in the normal state.

If, however, the cartilage is destroyed or displaced, the radiologist speaks of "joint space narrowing." Other irregularities may include effusion, which can be detected by an increase in soft-tissue density near the joint margin. So called **osteophytes** (chips of bones) are typically seen in the arthritic patient.

To summarize, the radiographic changes seen in arthritis includes:

1. So-called "lipping," "loose bodies," "spurs."

2. The joint space(s) may become irregular. With ensuing destruction of cartilage, the ends of the bones come into contact with each other, resulting in sclerosis or eburnation.

3. The so-called "loose bodies" which show up on x-rays are not really "loose" and free. They are attached to bone by fibrous strands.

Treatment:

Since osteo-arthritis is usually benign and is not a life-threatening condition, the prognosis is favorable.

Only in the case of spinal O.A. may there be severe disability. There are as many approaches to the treatment of O.A. as there are forms of arthritis.

1. Reassurance is important. The patient needs to be assured that while his condition may be painful at times, it should not be disabling, crippling, or fatal. The patient should be encouraged to maintain a vigorous and active lifestyle.

2. In severe cases, canes, crutches, walkers may be used to protect weight-bearing joints or body parts.

3. Different forms of physical therapy may be tried:

    a. A combination of heat and cold, hot packs, electric pads.

    b. Exercise: isometric to build power, isotonic to maintain motion. There are specific muscle group exercises, joint exercises which a physical therapist may prescribe to the patient.

4. Drug therapy may also be required. Drugs commonly used in the treatment of O.A. include aspirin, acetaminophen 600 mg (tylenol), propoxyphene, indocin, ibuprofen (motrin), feldene (the latter three belong to the class referred to as non-steroidal, antiinflammatories, N.S.A.I.s).

5. Intra-articular corticosteroids may be helpful on a short term basis, but are best reserved for acute

inflammatory flares. Muscle relaxants, such as diazepam (valium) 2 to 5 mg t.i.d. may be helpful.

6. Finally, as a last resort, surgery may be performed to remove the arthritic joint **in toto**. This is often done in certain knee and hip surgeries. In the case of foot surgery, the entire matarsophalangeal joint may be removed, the so-called **Keller** procedure. In the case of hammertoe surgery, the affected joint is removed, with some loss of function, and with almost total loss of the prior existing discomfort.

REFLEX SYMPATHETIC DYSTROPHY SYNDROME

REFLEX SYMPATHETIC DYSTROPHY SYNDROME

Reflex Sympathetic Dystrophy Syndrome (abbreviated R.S.D.S.) is a disorder of the sympathetic branch of the autonomic nervous system. The sympathetic branch of the autonomic nervous system regulates, in part, blood flow through the body. As a result of circulatory compromise to areas of the body, neurovascular changes occur, including hyperesthesias, paraesthesias, hyperhidrosis. Generally, R.S.D.S. follows some sort of trauma. Initially there may be some burning sensation to the area of trauma, and then after a period of time, there is severe pain, not in proportion to the triggering event.

R.S.D.S. can become progressively more severe, leading to trophic changes, including bone demineralization.

R.S.D.S., as a syndrome, refers to a host of possible conditions and states. For this reason, there are many names for the disorder, which include the following:

1. Acute inflammatory bone atrophy.

2. Acute bone atrophy.

3. Post traumatic pain syndrome.

4. Minor causalgia.

5. Post traumatic dystrophy.

6. Reflex sympathetic dystrophy.

7. Sudek's atrophy.

8. Reflex sympathetic dystrophy syndrome.

Clinical Aspects

As mentioned, characteristic of the syndrome is a neurovascular disorder. In over 90% of patients with R.S.D.S. pain in the extremity is the most common neurovascular finding. The pain is usually described as burning, aching, or throbbing. There may also be hypesthesia, hyperesthesia, or paraesthesia, swelling, and stiffness; also, hyperhidrosis (excessive perspiration).

As the syndrome progresses and becomes more severe, there are dystrophic changes, including thinning of the skin, demineralization of the bones (as seen on x-rays) a decrease in muscle volume, with resultant diminishment of motor function. When the bone demineralization is the predominent dystrophic change the condition is referred to as **Sudek's Atrophy**.

In the early stages of the condition, the patient complains of severe burning at the site of injury, often associated with warmth, edema, and hypertonic muscles. Later the edema may spread and the warm and flushed appearance gives way to a firm, cyanotic, and cool extremity, with increasingly stiff joints. Eventually the pain goes on to involve a larger area, and dystrophic changes of the bone predominate. The order of difficulties may vary, but generally in R.S.D.S. the neurovascular symptoms begin soon after the inciting trauma, and then after a period of time, the dystrophic changes begin to appear.

R.S.D.S. may begin after any of a number of different types of injuries such as sprains, soft-tissue wounds, fractures of varied severity, surgical procedures, and infection. A striking and characteristic feature of R.S.D.S. is that the neurovascular and dystrophic changes are increased out of proportion to the initial trauma. Long after the inciting traumatic episode (such as an ankle sprain) clinical changes involving edema, burning, aching, paraesthesias, etc. increase despite tissue healing. Recovery in R.S.D.S. can be slow, or, surprisingly enough, spontaneous.

X-ray changes suggestive of R.S.D.S. are seen most frequently in the short bones of the extremity. The early changes give the bone a mottle or patchy appearance. Later the bone may appear diffusely or sometimes markedly demineralized.

In addition to the physical manifestations of pain, burning, edema, hyperhidrosis, etc., there may also be psychiatric or psychologic distrubances involved in the pathogenesis of R.S.D.S. Since R.S.D.S. involves a disorder of the sympathetic nervous system (responsible for regulating body heat by vasoconstriction and vasodilation) there may also be personality changes or mood shifts either caused by the sympathetic nervous system or as a result of prolonged pain and disability. Patients with R.S.D.S. may also suffer from hysteria, psychoneurosis, depression, mood shifts, etc.

Treatment for R.S.D.S.

Ideally, the best way to treat R.S.D.S. is to prevent it from occuring. The doctor should be aware of the possibility of his patient developing this troublesome condition. After treatment for the inciting injury, **functional mobilization** yields the best result.

Specific, early therapy should include the use of mild analgesics and tranquilizers to relieve pain and anxiety. Physical therapy measures include local application of heat, baths, manual massage, normal range of motion exercises. Casts, braces, or forceful manipulations should not be used.

If a localized area of tenderness is present, repeated local anesthetic injections may be helpful. The primary treatment for the later stage of R.S.D.S. is interruption of the sympathetic nervous system. This can be done initially by the use of local anesthetics in and about the spinal canal. As a final resort, if all else fails, surgical sympathectomy may be performed. This is a drastic final step only in cases where all other treatment modalities have been used, with little or no success, and when the patient's symptoms are severe.

In summary, Reflex Sympathetic Dystrophy Syndrome, (R.S.D.S.) refers to a host of disorders involving a dysfunction of the sympathetic branch of the autonomic nervous system. The syndrome is triggered by an inciting injury (usually relatively minor, such as a sprain or strain) which may after a period of time heal on a tissue level, but persist on the neurovascular level. The syndrome can be diagnosed based on specific radiologic changes (thinning, demineralization of bone) and a clinical picture of neurovascular impairment. Because of the chronic and sometimes severe nature of the pain caused by R.S.D.S. patients may develop psychiatric disturbances, including malingering, hysteria, psychoneurosis, and depression.

The best way to treat R.S.D.S. is to prevent its occurrence. For this reason, even seemingly minor injuries should be treated vigorously and appropriately. In the early stages of treatment **functional mobilization** of the area yields best results. Later treatment modalities can include analgesics and tranquilizers, physical therapy, range of motion exercises, and local anesthetic injections. A final and last resort in severe, recalcitrant cases of R.S.D.S. is surgical sympathectomy.

DIABETES MELLITUS

DIABETES MELLITUS

Introduction

Aretaeus, the Greek physician, named the disease **diabetes** in the first century A.D. when he described a melting down of the flesh of limbs to urine.

Mellitus, the Greek word for honey, was added when, by taste and chemical analysis, a sweet substance was noted in the urine.

Although more than 50 years have elapsed since the discovery of **insulin** by Best and Banting, and despite worldwide clinical and laboratory research, we still have much to learn about the course of this disease, its pathophysiology, and treatment.

What is diabetes?

There are many definitions for this complex and terribly important disease state. Most experts seem to agree that the condition of diabetes, because of its complexity, is in fact more than a disease, just as cancer is more than one disease because of the variety of types of disease present.

It is for this reason that many experts prefer to call diabetes a **syndrome**. By **syndrome** we mean a set of symptoms characterizing a disease or condition, since not all symptoms need be present for the condition of diabetes to be diagnosed.

Now that we understand what is meant by **syndrome**, we are ready for the following working definition of diabetes.

Diabetes is a syndrome resulting from an interaction of hereditary and environmental factors, and characterized by abnormal insulin secretion and a variety of metabolic and vascular manifestations reflected in a tendency toward elevated blood glucose, in addition to:

    a. thickened capillary basal lamina.

    b. accelerated atherosclerosis.

    c. neuropathy.

The disorders caused by diabetes will be carefully examined shortly.

It is important to understand that diabetes is a biochemical disorder of carbohydrate, protein, and lipid metabolism. Classically, diabetes is characterized by **hyperglycemia** (elevated blood sugar) and glycosuria (sugar in the urine). The outward manifestations of diabetes, hyperglycemia and glycosuria are caused by the biochemical disorder within the body.

The central disturbance in the disease is an abnormality in secretion or action of insulin, or both. The insulin deficiency may be relative or absolute.

In the overwhelming number of instances, diabetes is genetically determined, but disorders of the pancreas, endocrine disorders, and viral infection may also cause diabetes.

What makes diabetes a syndrome rather than a disease, is its variable symptoms and unpredictable course of development. By variability and unpredictability, we refer to the following elements of this disorder.

1. There is no definitive etiology for diabetes.

2. Its pathogenesis – or course of development, is variable and often times unpredictable.

3. There are no specific laboratory tests.

4. Finally, and most important, there is no definitive or curative therapy at this time.

Despite its variability, indefinite etiology, and uncertain, unpredictable clinical course, most physicians agree that the **syndrome** of **diabetes** exists in a patient when there is:

1. An elevated fasting blood sugar (called hyperglycemia).

2. A decreased glucose tolerance.

As stated, although diabetes should accurately be called a **syndrome**, we shall refer to it henceforth as a disease since it is commonly referred to as such by both the lay and professional public.

Tenuous as our definition of diabetes has been, to complicate the matter further, diabetes has been further classified into three subgroups:

1. Prediabetes (potential diabetes).

2. Latent diabetes (chemical diabetes).

3. Overt diabetes.

Furthermore, there are two types of diabetes, maturity or adult onset diabetes, and juvenile diabetes.

The Diagnosis Of Diabetes

Although a number of tests may be utilized in the diagnosis of diabetes, the most commonly accepted one is the oral glucose tolerance test. This test is discussed in the chapter dealing with laboratory medicine. The test and its significance are discussed here, again, because of the great importance of this disease.

Although the oral glucose tolerance test is generally recognized, it is not an absolute or even a precise diagnostic marker. Currently, an elevation of fasting blood or plasma glucose is the most useful criterion for diagnosis. These values are so important they bear repetition.

The normal fasting glucose in venous plasma is between 60 and 110 mg/100 ml. and increases about 2 mg./100 ml. per decade after age 30.

"Normal" values as high as 140 mg/100 ml. may sometimes be seen in the elderly.

For the glucose tolerance test, fasting plasma glucose levels are measured 1 hour and 2 hours after a 75 gm oral glucose "load" has been given to the patient. Oftentimes a premeasured carbonated commercial preparation of glucose is given to the patient. When these test results are obtained, they are plotted against a chart of plasma glucose and age. The so-called "normal," "borderline" and "diabetes" results are based on so-called standardized test conditions and accepted values within the medical profession.

The glucose tolerance test, although relatively simple to administer, requires careful patient preparation and monitoring. Furthermore, a whole series of complicating conditions (such as pregnancy, systemic infection, myocardial infarction) must be ruled out by the physician to properly interpret the test results.

The test described here is the **two hour postprandial blood sugar determination** which is less expensive and more convenient to administer than the standard glucose tolerance test.

The two hour postprandial blood sugar determination is commonly used as a screening procedure. It places less stress on patients whose diabetes is moderate to markedly severe. When carbohydrate intolerance is mild, and when other metabolic conditions affecting sugar metabolism are to be studied, the **standard glucose tolerance test** is used. For the standard test, blood sugar is determined at fasting level, 30 minutes, 60, 90, 120, 180, and in certain cases, four, five, and six hours postload.

While the glucose tolerance test is relatively simple, its interpretation is complicated by factors such as:

1. Differing criteria for diagnosing diabetes by the test.

2. Lack of reliability in certain older individuals.

3. Lack of reproducibility in normal and diabetic patients.

4. Variability in method of laboratory analysis of blood samples.

Despite the flaws and shortcomings, the glucose tolerance test (both the standard form and the 2 hour post prandial) are here to stay as diagnostic criteria in determining diabetes. There are other tests used in the diagnosis of diabetes, and these include:

1. The intravenous glucose tolerance test.

2. The cortisone tolerance test.

3. The oral and intravenous tolbutamide tolerance test.

There are specific indications for these tests which are occasionally used for other metabolic disorders of sugar metabolism and diagnosing so-called "borderline" diabetic patients.

We have spent time looking at the glucose tolerance test, since it is often part of the definition of diabetes and is often used to diagnose the syndrome. The reader will recall that most physicians agree diabetes exists in a patient when there is:

1. An elevated fasting blood sugar (hyperglycemia).

2. A decreased glucose tolerance (that is, a positive glucose tolerance test).

Pathophysiology Of Diabetes

Pathophysiology refers to the course of a disease. There are several key features to the progression of this disease. Again, as is true of most syndromes, not all of these consequences of diabetes need be present for the serious effects of diabetes to be appreciated.

The pathophysiology of diabetes include these features:

1. Hyperglycemia

The hyperglycemia (elevated blood sugar level) is brought about by a relative or absolute lack of insulin secretion associated with an excess of circulating stress hormones (such as glucagon). The metabolic consequences of diabetes also include an alteration in lipid metabolism.

2. Large vessel disease

Many diabetic patients have an increased incidence, earlier onset, and increased severity of atherosclerosis in the intima and calcification in the media of the arterial wall.

3. Microvascular disease

Diabetics have an abnormality of the capillary basal lamina (basement membrane) characterized by added layers and increase thickness of the lamina. These changes usually occur in focal regions of the body, such as the legs and feet. Microvascular changes can also be found in the renal medulla, nervous system and heart.

4. Neuropathy

This is a very significant change. It involves segmental injury to nerves, associated with demyelination. Involved are the sensory and motor peripheral nerves and the autonomic nervous system. Microscopically, the affected nerves in a diabetic show basal lamina thickening similar to the capillary change of diabetes. Surprisingly, clinical signs of neuropathy (altered motor or sensory function) may precede symptoms of carbohydrate metabolism dysfunction (such as hyperglycemia).

5. Infection

There is an increased incidence of infection in the diabetic. The precise cause of this phenomenon is unknown. The combination of vascular impairment (large vessel and small vessel) and increased susceptibility to infection constitute a major problem for the diabetic patient.

6. Nephropathy

The diabetic has a predisposition to renal disease (kidney pathology). This means the kidney of the diabetic is subject to specific lesions, such as pyelonephritis, arterial nephrosclerosis, and papillary necrosis. The typical pathology of kidney disease in the diabetic is glomerulosclerosis. The advanced stage of diabetic glomerulosclerosis (also called Kimmelstiel–Wilson disease) involves:

a. A nephrotic syndrome.

b. Azotemia (elevated BUN blood levels) and is usually fatal.

7. Retinopathy

Diabetic retinopathy is the leading cause of blindness in the United States in adults under the age of sixty-five. The finding of diabetic retinopathy does not necessarily mean that blindness is imminent. All diabetics with ocular complications must be carefully monitored and treated if blindness is to be at all prevented. Unfortunately there is no satisfactory and definitive therapy for diabetic retinopathy. Treatment of all patients with retinopathy begins with an attempt to bring about strict control of the diabetes.

We have outlined the generally recognized chronic complications of diabetes, notably:

1. Nephropathy

Specifically, diabetic glomerulosclerosis, or Kimmelstiel-Wilson disease.

2. Retinopathy

Disease of the retina, which can, if the diabetes is uncontrolled or the patient is not carefully followed, lead to blindness.

3. Neuropathy

Sensory and motor impairment, particularly of the extremities, hands and feet.

In addition, the complications of diabetes include a number of biochemical structural, and functional abnormalities:

1. Large vessel disease.

2. Small vessel disease.

3. Susceptibility to infection.

We can now begin to appreciate the possible devastating effects of diabetes (the so-called chronic complications of diabetes).

The control of the blood sugar by diet and various antidiabetic therapy is a vital aspect in the care of diabetes, and hopefully, in the prevention of some of the possible chronic complications. It is these complications (nephropathy, retinopathy, neuropathy, infection, and others) which account for most diabetic morbidity and mortality.

We are now ready to examine, in a very general way, some aspects of the treatment and control of diabetes.

The Treatment And Control Of Diabetes

It is generally agreed to by most physicians that the goal in the treatment of diabetes is to keep symptoms of the disease under control, specifically by controlling hyperglycemia and glycosuria.

As is true in most aspects of medical practice, there are difficulties and complications associated with the treatment of this complex disease.

At this time, with the current state of the art in diabetes management, it is still unknown whether the treatment of asymptomatic hyperglycemia decreases morbidity and mortality. There is also significant risk in hypoglycemia in elderly patients given oral hypoglycemia agents or insulin therapy. Hypoglycemia and "insulin shock" are also adverse reactions which may occur in younger diabetic as a result of their diabetics medications.

There are currently three approaches in the management of diabetes. One or more of these approaches may be employed. The three treatments are:

1. Dietary treatment.

2. Oral hypoglycemia agents.

3. Insulin.

We shall now briefly examine each of these important modalities in the treatment or control of diabetes.

Dietary Treatment

Proper dietary management still remains the most important factor in the practical treatment of diabetes. For reasons that are still not understood, it is often the case that carbohydrate tolerance in the diabetic is diminished in the presence of obesity and frequently improves when normal body weight is achieved. Also, the response to oral hypoglycemic agents improves in the presence of normal body weight.

There is no "correct" dietary prescription for diabetics. Each diabetic is uniquely individual in his needs. The dietary treatment of any given diabetic, however, strives to:

1. Supply the total caloric requirement (carbohydrate, protein and fat) to maintain or achieve ideal body weight.

2. Satisfy special considerations, such as may occur in the presence of complications.

3. Provide adequate intake of vitamins and minerals.

When diet therapy begins, the physician may place the patient on a specific diet, or he may make a referral to a nutritional counselor. Consultations and evaluation are conducted at regular intervals to monitor the patient's management and control of the disease. Whether the diabetes is diet controlled alone, or controlled by medications, food intake by the patient is an integral part of the treatment.

Oral Hypoglycemia Agents

Since 1954 it has been possible to control diabetes in certain patients by the use of oral agents, to replace the inconvenience and difficulties associated with the injection therapy of insulin.

These oral agents, of which there are several brand names, belong to a chemical group called the **Sulfonylurea** compounds. The primary action of the sulfonylurea compounds is the stimulation of the pancreatic beta cells to secrete endogenous insulin.

Obviously, then, an oral hypoglycemia agent can only be used in the case of a diabetic who has functional beta cells in his pancreas which can be prompted by a sulfonylurea compound to produce enough useful insulin to satisfy the body's metabolic needs.

The physician must make the determination as to which diabetic patient would best benefit from the use of oral hypoglycemia agents vs. insulin. Since diabetes is subject to fluctuation, patients on sulfonylurea treatment must be regularly monitored by their physicians (and should also self-monitor at home by checking for sugar in their urine and by maintaining ideal body weight). The effects of dietary therapy should be evaluated in tandem with the sulfonylurea therapy.

Sulfonylurea therapy is a method of controlling the disease – it is **not** a cure. As stated in this chapter, unfortunately there is no cure for diabetes at this time, only attempts at maintaining control of this serious, potentially deadly disease.

Insulin

Insulin is a complex drug (hormone) commonly used in the treatment of diabetes. You will recall from our definition of diabetes, early in the chapter, that for diabetes to be present, there must be an abnormality either in the secretion of insulin or in its absorption by the cells of the body.

The purpose of **exogenous insulin** that is to say, insulin not produced from within the body, is to correct for the body's inability to produce or use its own (endogenous) insulin.

The correct use of insulin to treat the diabetic patient requires an extensive understanding of the hormone, its use and limitations.

The physician treating his diabetic patient with insulin must know a great deal about the chemistry and time activity of the various insulins; how they can be mixed; how they should be stored and handled, etc. The physician must be ever mindful of the various factors which may increase or decrease his patient's need for insulin. Finally, he must be aware of possible complications which may arise as a result of treatment with insulin. The patient who daily uses insulin also has a great responsibility in monitoring his response to his daily insulin dosage, strictly adhering to his dietary regimen, properly administering, storing, and handling his insulin.

It is beyond the scope of this book to examine the many elements involved in the use of insulin for diabetic treatment. The reader, however, should be aware that there are several types of insulin commonly available; there are special characteristics of the various insulins with respect to their action, peak effect, duration, and specific indications. There are also several important considerations with respect to the storage, handling, and administration of insulin in the treatment of diabetes, but which are beyond the scope of this chapter.

Ultimately, the goal of treatment in diabetes, whether that treatment involves diet alone, hypoglycemic agent alone, or insulin, is to maintain normal fasting blood glucose levels, "ideal" body weight; and the absence of glucosuria (urine sugar).

The Podiatrist's role in the care of diabetic patients:

Podiatrists have been debriding mycotic nails and treating excrescences (corns and calluses) of diabetic patients for many years.

We need to now examine the role of the podiatrist in the care of diabetic foot problems, and the precautions the podiatrist needs to take if the doctor is to avoid problems for himself (namely, malpractice suit) and his patient (loss of function or use, or ultimately death).

Diagnosis

In the chapter dealing with laboratory medicine we have already discussed the various standard tests used to detect the presence of diabetes. These tests include a urinalysis and fasting blood sugar test. Even before any such test is ordered, however, the podiatrist may well be the first member of the medical team to suspect the presence of diabetes. Since many diabetics develop early arteriosclerosis, a visual and palpatory examination may be enough to make the podiatrist suspect the existence of diabetes.

The podiatrist may request a urine specimen test in his office or even a blood glucose test for patients he suspects might be diabetics. While the tests are not definitive, they certainly can be helpful in determining whether further medical workup and care are needed.

Examination of the patient (physical examination).

The podiatrist is trained to evaluate skin color of the

feet, temperature, pulses, circulatory status, signs of vascular disorders (e.g. color and texture of nails), various dermatologic entities, neurologic status, and a host of other conditions which may be present in diabetes. Most of these signs involve simple observations; others are more involved, requiring special equipment, such as an oscillometer or a doppler to evaluate circulatory status.

In any event, the podiatrist has been well trained in school and in postgraduate exposure, to look for the signs and symptoms of the diabetic foot.

The classic signs of the diabetic foot include: thick, dry, compacted skin, lack of feeling to foot, poor to non-existent pedal pulses and thick, irregular fungal nails.

Diabetic Ulcer:

The podiatrist is frequently the first health care provider contacted by the patient with an ulcer of the foot or lower extremity. There are many causes of foot and leg ulcers. Before proceeding with any treatment course, the podiatrist should first ascertain the cause of the ulcer, caused by diabetes, or tuberculosis, or syphilis, sickle cell disease or by any number of possible diseases.

Once the podiatrist has established that the ulcer is secondary to diabetes, he must strive to have the patient's diabetes controlled. Ulcerations in diabetics will rarely heal if the underlying diabetes is not controlled. Controlling the diabetes is paramount in obtaining the desired clinical results required for the healing process. The podiatrist must, therefore, communicate with the patient's physician to make certain there is proper control of the diabetes.

Classically, there is no pain associated with the diabetic ulcer, which is what makes the condition more serious for the patient. Unchecked and if progressive, a diabetic ulcer can penetrate by means of sinuses in the foot into bones (typically the weight bearing areas of the foot; the metatarsals) resulting in osteomyelitis (infection of the bone, which can lead to the loss of the leg). An osteomyelitis in a diabetic can also have a fatal outcome.

Therapy

Preventive or prophylactic treatment is the ideal form of therapy for the diabetic foot patient.

Almost all of us at one time or another develop minor lesions of the foot, or occasional indwelling, or ingrown toenails. In the diabetic, because of his metabolic imbalance, which predisposes him towards infection, a minor foot lesion can develop into a major one. Thus, a simple corn, callus, or ingrown toenail can become a major problem. How many times have we heard the horror story of a diabetic family member who cut his own corn, or nails, developed an infection, lost a leg, and ultimately died?

While unfortunately there are instances of podiatrists who may have "nicked" a non-diabetic patient, the likelihood of such a patient developing a severe life-threatening infection as a result of such a podiatric treatment is remote. This is not the same when dealing with a diabetic, assuming there are no other compromising conditions in the body, such as P.V.D. (peripheral vascular disease). Because of the likelihood of infection as a result of self-administered home care (or care by other family members) it is best if the diabetic have a course of regular and ongoing foot treatment by a podiatrist to maintain a healthy pair of feet. The maintenance of good foot health in the controlled diabetic usually consists of cutting nails and removing corns and calluses. For a diabetic's good foot health, it is imperative that the patient be treated by a podiatrist on a regular, ongoing basis.

Ulcer Treatment By The Podiatrist

The podiatrist sees a great many diabetic ulcers. Most ulcers occur on points of pressure. It is essential, therefore, to prevent pressure to the area of the ulcer, also, as stated earlier, it is essential to attempt to maintain normal or near normal blood sugar levels. The local ulcer therapy of the podiatrist, no matter how fine, is doomed to failure if the underlying systemic problem of diabetes is not controlled.

It is beyond the scope of this book to go into the specifics of podiatric ulcer therapy. A great deal has been written in the professional literature on the subject. Proper treatment of diabetic foot ulcer includes the following elements:

1.   Eliminate weight bearing to affected area of foot.

2.   Improve blood flow
     (this may include the need for surgery, such as an arterial bypass).

3.   Provide topical care.

4.   Treat the infection.

5.   Control blood glucose levels.

In addition to treating the ulcer locally, the podiatrist may decide to institute internal medication for infection. At this point the podiatrist will need to determine if there is a drug sensitivity, circulatory, neurologic, or other condition which would preclude the use of any antibiotic medication. He should also base the use of an antibiotic he prescribes on the results of one or more culture and sensitivity studies of the ulcer (see lab section for description of C & S test). Furthermore, at all times the podiatrist should be checking to make certain the patient's underlying diabetic condition is under control.

Podiatric Surgery And The Diabetic Patient

Foot surgery on a diabetic patient must be approached with great care and circumspection. Many podiatrists refuse to operate on a diabetic patient, period. Other podiatrists will operate on the diabetic but only in a hospital setting, even for the so called minor or trivial procedure, such as an infected ingrown toenail.

In a well controlled diabetic, whose blood sugar results, chemistry profile, urinalysis, other laboratory results and circulating status are within normal limits, there should not be a great fear on the part of the surgeon-podiatrist or patient to proceed with a podiatric surgical procedure. If pulses are present, and if digital vascular tests, oscillometric readings, temperature, skin and nail texture are normal, and all the other preoperative criteria of otherwise healthy, normal patients are present, there should be no problem with proceeding with a planned operation of the foot. However, it is important that the patient's underlying metabolic disorder (his diabetes) be carefully monitored at all times, preoperative, intra-operatively, and postoperatively to prevent, for example, a hyperglycemia, exacerbated by the stress of surgery, anesthesia, or infection. Hyperglycemia could lead to dehydration and other complications which the surgeon would well want to avoid.

In conclusion, the podiatrist, as the foot specialist, plays an integral and vital role in the care of diabetic patients, both for prophylactic (routine-maintenance care) and emergency care (treatment of ulcers and infection).

The podiatrist may also perform elective surgery (non-emergency basis) on the diabetic patient whose diabetes is under control and who has normal or near normal vascular and neurologic status.

Since diabetes is a systemic disease with profound systemic consequences, it is essential that the podiatrist be ever mindful of the patient's overall health status when treating what appears to be, on the surface, a very local foot problem. The podiatrist should attempt to maintain lines of communication with the patient's internist and other physicians who are monitoring the diabetic's health status. It is the podiatrist's responsibility and in keeping with the standards of podiatric community care.

OSTEOMYELITIS

OSTEOMYELITIS

Osteomyelitis is the inflammation of bone caused by a pyogenic organism.

Traditionally when doctors speak of osteomyelitis they refer to two types of osteomyelitis: the acute and chronic forms.

Let us first look at the **acute** form of this disease. The etiology (or cause) of acute osteomyelitis may be divided into hematogenous and post-traumatic. Hematogenous osteomyelitis is relatively rare in the bones of the foot. We need not concern ourselves with this relatively uncommon form of osteomyelitis, but should be aware of its existence. The **posttraumatic** form of osteomyelitis is more common in the foot. The organism gains access to the bony tissues by direct extension, as from ulcers, open fractures, and postsurgery. The infecting organism (usually bacterial) does not spread as rapidly to involve the entire bone as in hematogenous osteomyelitis because an immediate drainage passage is usually available.

The **posttraumatic** form of osteomyelitis also differs from hematogenous osteomyelitis in that it is not associated with the extreme systemic signs of toxicity. We shall discuss these signs of osteomyelitis shortly.

Further general remarks on osteomyelitis

In the **acute form** of osteomyelitis we see the following systemic manifestations:

1.   Fever.

2.   Malaise – (generalized weakness, fatigue).

3. Leukocytosis – (elevated white blood count).

4. Intense pain in the affected area.

5. The following classic triad:

   a. sepsis (infection).
   b. local pain.
   c. local tenderness.

In the **Chronic form** of osteomyelitis we find the following:

1. Local low grade infection.

2. Drainage from cutaneous sinus.

3. Episodic pain.

4. Erythema (redness).

5. Edema (swelling).

The acute and chronic forms of osteomyelitis are sometimes also referred to as suppurative, meaning that pus is produced.

The question arises, how does this serious condition called **osteomyelitis** develop in the body? Generally, there are two ways:

1. Postsurgical.

2. Nonsurgical, usually posttrauma.

The postsurgical cause of osteomyelitis is generally because of postoperative infection. Postoperative infection may be caused by any number of factors, including:

1. Poor or improper surgical technique.

2. Nonsterile surgery and postoperative care.

3. Kirshner wire and foreign body, including silastic implants and other hardware.

Pathophysiology

We now need to look a little more closely at the course of this disease, its **pathophysiology**. Generally, in most forms of osteomyelitis and regardless of the causative factor, an **embolus** is dislodged.

1. This embolus, which is a clot or other plug obstructing a blood vessel, will enter the bone via a nutrient artery.

2. The embolus may then become entrapped in the micro vessels of the bone, creating a bony infarction. An infarct is an area of necrosis due to local ischemia commonly caused by a thrombus or embolus.

3. An infarct usually leads to **ischemia** (shut off of blood supply to an area) and subsequent **necrosis** (tissue death).

4. The body tries to protect itself from necrotic tissue by having a reactive hyperemia (increased temperature) along with polymorphonuclear cyst formation.

5. The affected bone starts becoming demineralized.

6. Tissue debris starts forming as a result of bone destruction (caused by proteolytic enzymes) leading to compression of micro- vessels causing

further bone necrosis.

7. Some of this necrotic exudate goes through the Haversian canals and emerges beneath the periosteum.

8. The periosteum begins to push up, attempting to wall off the infection by forming new bones (this process of new bone formation by periosteal elevation is called **involucrum**).

9. If left unhindered, the infectious process continues with greater thrombosis and inflammatory reaction; eventually the necrotic bone tissue separates, forming what is called a **sequestrum**.

10. Sinus tract may be present to the skin surface (sometimes called a **cloaca**).

11. In certain instances, the initial infection becomes walled off by inflammatory fibrous tissue, creating a localized abscess that may undergo spontaneous sterilization or become a chronic nidus of infection (called a **Brodie's abscess**).

Clinical Diagnosis:

Now that we know something about the destruction which osteomyelitis can cause, we can better appreciate some of the clinical signs present in the disease.

In the case of the **acute hematogenous** form of osteomyelitis there is usually an acute systemic febrile illness, accompanied by the following signs:

1. Fever.

2. Local pain.

3. Erythema (redness).

4. Edema (swelling).

5. Anorexia (loss of appetite).

6. Lethargy.

7. Possible septicemia (blood infection).

Blood cultures, if taken, may turn out positive during this stage. Any necrosis of bone is usually not sufficiently advanced to be demonstrable on x-rays for the first seven to ten days following onset of the infection. Although spontaneous healing may occur, the usual course in the absence of adequate therapy is towards chronicity, with destruction of bone and the risk of metastatic dissemination of the infection.

In the case of the **chronic** form of osteomyelitis (again, also usually caused by hematogenous spread) we find the following signs:

1. Low grade fever.

2. Sub-clinical symptoms.

3. Blood culture may or may not be positive.

4. Usually chronic osteomyelitis is found in persons over the age of 30 and not in children.

5. Clinical signs are basically vague.

A chronic osteomyelitis may develop from a lingering pocket of infection originally caused by an acute attack, which over a period of many years remained dormant or subclinical. This is one reason why the vigorous and thorough treatment of any form of osteomyelitis is so important to prevent a chronic, subclinical osteomyelitis from developing.

X-Rays (Radiographic changes)

In addition to the signs and symptoms of osteomyelitis already enumerated, there are several x-ray changes which help the clinician arrive at this diagnosis.

1. Soft tissue swelling, especially near bone. This is a deep swelling, where muscle fiber integrity is destroyed.

2. With very clear x-rays it may be possible to see areas of rarefaction and mottling on the metaphysis of bones.

3. A raised periosteum is one classic sign for osteomyelitis.

4. In the acute state of the disease, certainly for the first 7 to 10 days following infection, there are no radiographic changes.

5. As the disease progresses we see a "moth eaten" appearance that is, a mingling of destroyed and healthy tissue.

6. Eventually, there is bone necrosis and bone fragments evident (**sequestrum**).

7. Osteoblastic activity continues and there will be calcification about a cortex. This is new bone formation, referred to as **involucrum**. (Note, it is possible to have a **sequestrum** within an **involucrum**).

Treatment

It is beyond the scope of this chapter to take up all elements of treatment for this serious condition. A few general remarks are indicated however.

1. Proper treatment of chronic osteomyelitis begins with the identification of the offending organism.

2. Cultures should be taken of the draining sinus and IV antibiotics started.

3. X-rays should be taken to visualize the areas of necrotic bone.

4. Once the area of involvement is well delineated the lesion is incised and drained.

5. All necrotic soft tissue is debrided and the bone curretted until all sequestrum are removed and the bone is freely bleeding.

6. The wound is immobilized, and constantly irrigated until cultures are negative.

7. Once the infection is resolved, if there is tissue deficit, reconstructive plastic surgery may be contemplated, i.e. skin and bone grafting.

In summary, osteomyelitis is a serious infective process which needs to be diagnosed at its early stages and treated promptly and vigorously.

PODIATRIC VOCABULARY AND DEFINITIONS

PODIATRIC VOCABULARY & DEFINITIONS

The object of this Chapter is to give the reader a working knowledge of terms, definitions and terminology of the most commonly used words in the podiatric field.

– A –

Abduct	To move the foot away from the median line of the body.
Abduction	The movement of the foot away from the median line of the body.
Abscess	A circumscribed collection of pus that appears in an acute or chronic phase, localized infection, and associated with tissue destruction and most commonly, swelling.
Acute	Of short duration and short course of occurrence, used in association with disease.
Adduct	To move the foot toward the median line of the body.
Adduction	The movement of the foot toward the median line of the body.
Adhesion	This is the process of uniting or adhering of two surfaces or parts, specifically the union of the opposing surfaces of a wound.
Adrenaline	Epinephrine.

Aerobe	A microorganism that thrives, lives and/or grows in the presence of oxygen.
Aerobic	Living in air, aerophilic; aerophilous.
Afebrile	Apyretic; No temperature.
Allergic	To relate to any response stimulated by an allergen.
Allergy	An acquired sensitivity; an immunologic state that is induced in a subject who is susceptible to an antigen (allergen), which is characterized by a marked change in the subject's reactivity.
Ambulatory	Walking about or ability to walk about.
Amputation	The cutting off of a foot, part of a foot or lower limb.
Amputee	A person who has had an amputation.
Anaerobe	A microorganism that thrives, lives and/or grows in the absence of oxygen.
Anaerobic	Living in the absence of oxygen.
Analgesia	A condition where nociceptive stimuli are perceived but not interpreted as pain.
Analgesic	A chemical compound which has the capability of producing analgesia, re-

lief of pain.

Analgetic
An analgesic; associated with altered pain perception.

Anaphylactoid
Relating to anaphylaxis manifesting extremely great sensitivity to foreign protein or other material.

Anaphylaxis
A term which indicates a lessened resistance to a toxin which results from a previous inoculation of the same material, and in this sense was synonymous with hypersensitivity in its original usage of a postulated increase sensitivity to a toxin.

Anemia
Any condition in which the number of red blood cells per cubic mm, the amount of hemoglobin in 100 ml of blood, and the volume of packed red blood cells per 100 ml are less than normal.

Anemic
Pertaining to or manifestating the various features of anemia.

Anesthesia
A state characterized by loss of sensation, the result of pharmacological depressions of nerve function or of neurological disease.

Anesthesiologist
A physician who specializes solely in anesthesiology and related areas.

Anesthesiology
The medical specialty concerned with the pharmacological, physiological, and clinical basis of anesthesia and related fields, including resuscitation, intensive respira-

tory care, and pain.

Anesthetic	An anesthetic agent: a compound that reversibly depresses neuronal function, producing loss of ability to perceive pain and/or sensations.
Anesthetist	A person who administers an anesthetic, whether an anesthesiologist, a physician who is not an anesthesiologist, a nurse anesthetist, etc.
Anesthetize	To produce loss of sensation.
Ankle	The joint between the leg and foot in which the tibia and fibula above articulate with the talus below.
Ankylosis	Stiffening of a joint.
Anterior	Before, in relation to time or space. Ventral; ventralis; in human anatomy denoting the front surface of the body.
Antero	A prefix denoting anterior.
Anteroposterior	Relating to both front and rear. In x-ray describing the path of the beam from anterior to posterior through the patient to expose the film, e.g. an A-P view of the foot.
Antibiotic	A soluble substance derived from a mold, or synthetically in the laboratory bacteria that inhibits the growth of other microorganisms. **Broad Spectrum** - one having a wide range of activity against both Gram

positive and Gram negative microorganisms.

Anti-inflammatory
Reducing inflammation by acting on body mechanisms. Examples of antiinflammatory agents are antihistamines and glucocorticoids.

Artery
A blood vessel conveying blood in a direction away from the heart.

Arthritis
Articular rheumatism; inflammation of a joint; state characterized by inflammation of joints.

Arthrodesis
Artificial ankylosis; syndesis, the stiffening of a joint by operative means.

Arthrogram
An x-ray of a joint; usually infers the introduction of a contrast agent into the joint capsule.

Arthropathy
Arthropathia; any disease affecting a joint.

Arthroplasty
The making of an artificial joint. An operation to restore as far as possible the integrity and functional power of a joint.

Articulation
A joining or connecting together loosely so as to allow motion between the parts.

Ataxia
The inability to perform coordinated muscular movement.

Avulsion
A tearing away or forcible separation; as in removal of a nail.

Babinski phenomenon   The extension of the great toe and abduction reflex or sign of the other toes instead of the normal flexion to plantar stimulation, considered indicative of pyramidal tract involvement ("positive" Babinski).

Bandage   A piece of cloth or other material of varying shape and size, applied to a body part to make compression, absorb drainage, prevent motion or retain surgical dressings.

Bilateral   Relating to, or having, two sides.

Biomechanics   The science of the action of forces, internal or external, on the living body.

Biopsy   The process of removing tissue from living patients for diagnostic examination.

Biped   Two footed.

Bipedal   Relating to a biped. Capable of locomotion on two feet.

Blister   A fluid-filled vesicle under the epidermis or within the epidermis.

Blood   The fluid and its suspended formed elements that are circulated through the heart, arteries, capillaries and veins.

Blood Count	Calculation of the number of red (RBC) or white (WBC) blood cells in a cubic millimeter of blood.
Bone	A hard tissue consisting of cells in a matrix of ground substance and collagen fibers. The fibers are impregnated with mineral substance, chiefly calcium phosphate and carbonate.
Bruise	Contusion; an injury usually producing a hematoma without rupture of the skin.
Bunion	A localized swelling of either the medial or dorsal aspect of the first metatarsophalangeal joint, caused by an inflammatory bursa; the medical bunion usually associated with a hallux valgus.
Bunionectomy	The excision of a bunion.
Bunionette	A localized swelling at either the lateral or dorsal aspect of the fifth metatarsophalangeal joint, caused by an inflammatory bursa; the lateral bunion usually called a Tailor's bunion.
Bur	A rotatory cutting instrument used in podiatry, consisting of a head and a small shaft of steel or other hard metal. It is designed in various end shapes and is used at various rotational velocities to shave or smooth down bone.
Burn	A lesion caused by heat or any cau-

terizing agent.

Bursa   A closed sac or envelope lined with synovia and containing fluid, usually found or formed in areas subject to friction.

– C –

Calcaneus   The heel bone; os calcis; the largest of the tarsal bones.

Calcification   A process in which tissue or noncellular material in the body becomes hardened as the result of precipitates or larger deposits of insoluble salts of calcium.

Calcify   To deposit or lay down calcium salts, as in the formation of bone.

Callosity   Callus, keratoma or tyloma. A circumscribed thickening of the keratin layer of the epidermis as a result of friction or intermittent pressure.

Callous   Relating to callus or callosity.

Callus   Callosity. The hard boneline substance that develops between and around the ends of a fractured bone.

Calor   Heat, as one of the four signs of inflammation.

Capsular   Relating to any capsule.

Capsule   A fibrous tissue layer enveloping a tumor, especially if benign.

Carbolic Acid	Phenol.
Cartilage	A connective tissue characterized by its nonvascularity and firm consistency.
Cartilaginous	Chondral; relating to or consisting of cartilage.
Cast	The rigid encasement of a part for purposes of immobilization.
Causalgia	Persistent severe burning sensation of the skin, usually following direct or indirect (vascular) injury of sensory fibers of a peripheral nerve, and accompanied by cutaneous changes.
Cautery	An agent or device used for scarring, burning, or cutting the skin or tissues by means of heat, electric current, or caustic chemicals.
Cellulitis	The inflammation of cellular or connective tissue.
Chiropodist	Podiatrist.
Chiropody	Podiatry.
Cicatrix	Scar.
Circulation	(Blood). The course of the blood from the heart through the arteries, capillaries, and veins back again to the heart.
Circulatory	Relating to the circulation.

Clamp	An instrument for compression of a structure.
Claudication	Intermittent: a condition caused by ischemia of the muscles due to sclerosis with narrowing of the arteries. It is characterized by attacks of lameness and pain, brought on by walking, chiefly in the calf muscles.
Clavus	Corn, heloma: a small conical callosity caused by pressure over a bony prominence.
Clonus	A form of movement marked by contractions and relaxations of a muscle, occurring in rapid succession.
Clubbing	A condition affecting the toes in which the extremities of the digits are broadened, and the nails are abnormally curved longitudinally and are shiny.
Clubfoot	Talipes equinovarus.
Comminuted	Broken into fragments; denoting especially a fractured bone.
Complaint	A malady, disease or symptom, or the description of it.
Complication	A morbib process or event occurring during a disease which is not an essential part of the disease, although it may result from it or from independent causes.
Condylectomy	Excision of a condyle.

Congenital	Existing at birth; may be due to hereditary factors.
Conservative	Denoting treatment by gradual, limited or well established procedure.
Consultant	A physician or surgeon who does not take actual charge of a patient, but acts in an advisory capacity deliberating with and counseling the doctor of record.
Consultation	Meeting of two or more physicians to evaluate the nature and progress of disease in a particular patient and to establish diagnosis, prognosis, and therapy.
Corn	Hard corn, heloma durum; the form of corn over a toe joint. Soft corn, heloma molle, a corn formed by pressure between two toes, the surface being macerated and yellowish in color.
Cortex	The outer portion of an organ or bone as distinguished from the inner, or medullary portion.
Culture	The propagation of microorganism on or in media of various kinds.
Curettage	Curettement; a scraping for the removal of new growths or other abnormal tissues or to obtain material for tissue diagnosis.
Cyst	An abnormal sac containing gas, fluid, or a semisolid material, with a membranous lining.

Deformity | Deformation; a deviation from the normal shape or size, resulting in disfigurement; may be congenital or acquired.

Degeneration | Deteriorating; sinking from a higher to a lower level or type.

Dehiscence | A bursting open, splitting, or gaping along natural or sutured lines.

Demineralization | A loss or decrease of the mineral constituents of the body or individual tissues, especially of bone.

Dermatitis | Inflammation of the skin.

Diabetes | Either diabetes insipidus or diabetes mellitus, diseases having in common the symptom polyuria. When used without qualification, it means diabetes mellitus.

Diagnose | The determination of the nature of a disease.

Digit | Finger or toe.

Disease | Morbus: illness, sickness, an interruption, cessation, or disorder of body functions, systems, or organs.

Dislocation | Luxation: displacement of an organ or any part specifically a disturbance or disarrangement of the normal relation of the bones entering into the formation of a joint.

Disorder — A disturbance of function, structure, or both resulting from a genetic or embrylogic failure in development or from exogenous factors such as poison, injury or disease.

Distal — Situated away from the center of the body, or from the point of origin; specifically applied to the extremity or distant part of a limb.

Dolor — Pain, as one of the four signs of inflammation.

Dorsiflexion — Turning of the foot or the toes upward.

Dosage — The giving of medicine or other therapeutic agent in prescribed amounts.

Drainage — The continuous withdrawal of fluids from a wound.

Dressing — The material applied, or its application, to a wound for protection, absorbance, drainage, etc.

Drug — A therapeutic agent; any substance, other than food, used in the prevention, diagnosis alleviation, treatment, or cure of disease or disease entity.

Dysfunction — Difficult or abnormal function.

Edema	An accumulation of an excessive amount of watery fluid cells, tissues, or serious cavities. A swelling of tissues.
Epinephrine	Adrenaline.
Erythema	Inflammatory redness of the skin.
Eschar	A thick, coagulated crust of slough which develops following a thermal burn or chemical or physical cauterization of the skin.
Etiology	The science and study of the causes of disease and their mode of operation.
Evert	To turn the bottom of the foot outward.
Eversion	A turning outward of the bottom of the foot.
Exacerbation	An increase in the severity of a disease or any of its signs or symptoms.
Extend	To straighten a limb; to diminish or extinguish the angle formed by flexion; to place the distal segment of a limb in such a position that its axis is continuous with that of the proximal segment.
Extension	The act of bringing the distal portion of a joint in continuity with the long axis of the proximal portion.

Extensor	A muscle the contraction of which tends to straighten a limb; the antagonist of a flexor.
Exudate	Any fluid that has exuded out of a tissue or its capillaries, more specifically because of injury or inflammation.

– F –

Fascia	A sheet of fibrous tissue that envelops the body beneath the skin; it also encloses muscles and groups of muscles, and separates their several layers or groups.
Fasciitis	Inflammation in fascia.
Fascitis	Fasciitis.
Fat–pad	An accumulation of somewhat encapsulated adipose tissue.
Femoral	Relating to the femur or thigh.
Femur	The thigh bone.
Fever	A bodily temperature above the normal of 98.6°F (37°C).
Flatfoot	**Talipes Planus, pes planus.**
Flex	To bend: to move a joint in such a direction as to approximate the two parts which it corrects.
Flexion	The act of flexing or bending e.g.

bending of a joint so as to approximate the part it connects.

Flexor — A muscle the action of which is to flex a joint.

Flush — To wash out with a full stream of fluid.

Forceps — An instrument for seizing a structure, and making compression or traction.

Forefoot — The front part of the foot.

Fracture — To break. A break, especially the breaking of a bone or cartilage.

Fungistatic — Mycostatic: having an inhibiting action upon the growth of fungi.

Fungus — A general term used to encompass the diverse morphological forms of yeasts and molds.

– G –

Gait — A manner of walking.

Gangrene — Mortification: necrosis due to obstruction, loss, or diminution of blood supply; it may be localized to a small area or involve an entire extremity or organ and may be wet or dry.

Gangrenous — Mortified: relating to or affected with gangrene.

Gout — A metabolic disorder, occurring

especially in men, characterized by a raised but variable blood uric acid level, recurrent acute arthritis of sudden onset, deposition of crystalline sodium urate in connective tissues and articular cartilage and progressive chronic arthritis.

Graft | Any free (unattached) tissue or organ for transplantation.

Granulation | The formation of minute, and may be rounded, fleshy connective tissue projections on the surface of a wound, ulcer, or inflamed tissue surface in the process of healing.

– H –

Haglund's Deformity
or Disease | An abnormal prominence of the posterior superior lateral aspect of the calcaneus (os calcis), caused by a disturbance of gait.

Hallux | The great toe. The first digit of the foot.

Hallux flexus | Hammertoe involving the first toe.

Hallux rigidus | Stiff toe, a condition in which there is a stiffness in the first metatarsophalangeal joint, the joint may be the site of a hypertrophic arthritis.

Hallux valgus | A deviation of the tip of the first toe, or main axis of the toe, toward the outer or lateral side of the foot.

Hallux varus	A deviation of the tip of the first toe, or main axis of the toe, toward the inner or medial side of the foot.
Hammertoe	A deformity of any toe in which the proximal phalanx is dorsiflexed on the metatarsal head, the middle phalanx is plantar flexed, and the distal phalanx is flexed or extended.
Heloma	Clavus, corn.
Heloma durum	Hard corn.
Heloma molle	Soft corn.
Hematoma	A localized mass of extravasated blood that is relatively or completely confined within an organ or tissue, a space or a potential space.
Hemostasis	The arrest of bleeding.
Hyperemia	The presence of an increased amount of blood in a part or organ.
Hyperesthesia	Oxyesthesia: abnormal acuteness of sensitivity to touch, pain, or other sensory stimuli.
Hyperextension	Overextension: superextension; extension of a limb or part beyond the normal limit.
Hyperglycemia	An abnormally high concentration of glucose in the circulating blood.
Hyperhidrosis	Excessive or profuse sweating.

Hypermobility	Increased range of movement of joints, joint laxity, occurring normally in children or as a result of disease.
Hyperostosis	Hypertrophy of bone. Exostosis.
Hypertension	High blood pressure.
Hypertensive	Marked by an increased blood pressure.
Hypertrophy	A general increase in bulk of a part or organ not due to tumor formation.
Hypoglycemia	An abnormally small concentration of glucose in the circulating blood.

– I –

Iatrogenic	An adverse condition which is induced by therapeutic effort itself.
Incision	A cut, a division of the soft parts made with a surgical scalpel.
Inferior	Situated below or directed downward. In relationship to the foot, situated nearer the soles of the feet.
Inflammation	A fundamental pathologic process consisting of a dynamic complex of cytologic and histologic reactions that occur in the affected blood vessels and adjacent tissue in response to an injury or abnormal stimulation caused by physical, chemical, or biologic agent.

Inject	To introduce into the body denoting a fluid forced into one of the cavities, beneath the skin, or into a blood vessel.
Injectable	Capable of being injected into anything such as a syringe.
Injection	The introduction of a medicinal substance or nutrient material into the subcutaneous cellular tissue.
Injure	To wound, hurt or harm.
Injury	The damage or wound of trauma.
Inlay	A device inserted into a shoe.
Innervation	The supply of nerve fibers functionally connected with a part.
Insertion	The attachment of a muscle to the more movable part of the skeleton.
Interdigit	That part of the sloping extremity of the foot lying between any two adjacent toes.
Interphalangeal	Between two phalanges; denoting toe joints.
Interspace	Any space between the two adjoining objects.
Inversion	A turning inward of the bottom of the foot.
Invert	To turn the bottom of the foot inward.

Ischemia	Local anemia due to mechanical obstruction of the blood supply.
Ischemic	Relating to or affected by ischemia.

– J –

Joint	The movable place or articulation or part where two bones join.

– K –

Keloid–Cheloid	A nodular, frequently lobulated, firm, movable, nonencapsulated, generally linear mass of hyperplastic scar tissue.
Keratosis	Any lesion on the epidermis marked by the presence of circumscribed overgrowths of the horny layer.

– L –

Laser	A device which concentrates high energies into a narrow beam of coherent (nonspreading) monochromatic light.
Lateral	On the side. Farther from the median or midsagittal plane. In podiatry, a position either right or left of the midsagittal plane.
Latero	Combining from meaning lateral, to

one side, or relating to a side.

Lesion	A wound or injury. A pathological change in the tissue.
Ligament	A band or sheet of fibrous tissue connecting two or more bones, cartilage, or other structures, or serving as support for fasciae or muscles.
Lipedema	Chronic swelling, usually of the lower extremities: caused by the widespread, even distribution of subcutaneous fat and fluid.
Lipoma	An adipose tumor; a benign neoplasm of adipose tissue, comprised of mature fat cells.
Longitudinal	Running lengthwise; in the direction of the long axis of the body or any of its parts.

– M –

Macerate	To soften.
Maceration	Softening by the action of a liquid.
Malady	Disease; illness.
Malalignment	The malpositioning of one structure to another.
Malformation	Failure of proper or normal development.
Malfunction	Disordered, inadequate or abnormal

function.

Malpractice	The mistreatment of a disease, surgery or injury through ignorance, carelessness, or criminal intent or deviation from the standard of community care.
Malunion	Incomplete union, or union in a faulty position, after fracture of a wound of the soft parts.
Matrix	The formative portion of a nail.
Matrixectomy	Destruction of nail matrix cells by surgical intervention.
Medicate	To treat a medical condition by the giving of drugs. To impregnate with a medicinal substance.
Medication	The act of medicating. A medicinal substance.
Metatarsal	Relating to any one of the five long bones of the foot.
Metatarsalgia	Pain in the forefoot in the region of the heads of the metatarsals.
Metatarsophalangeal	Relating to the articulation between the metatarsal bones and the phalanges.
Metatarsus	The distal portion of the foot between the instep and the toes, having as its skeleton the five long bones (metatarsal bones) articulating posteriorly with the cuboid and cuneiform bones and distally with

the phalanges.

Metatarsus Adductovarus	Same deformity as above, (same basic pathology) with the deformity occurring principally on the frontal plane.
Metatarsus Adductus	A deformity in the transverse plane, whereby the metatarsals are angulated towards the midline of the axis at a higher degree than normal.
Metatarsus Varus	Intoe: fixed deformity of the foot in which the forepart of the foot is rotated on the long axis of the foot, so that the plantar surface faces the midline of the body.
Motile	Having the power of spontaneous movement.
Motility	The power of spontaneous movement.
Muscle	A discrete bundle or sheet or sheath of contractile fibers having the function of producing movement.
Myasthenia	Muscular weakness.
Mycosis	Any disease caused by a fungus or yeast.
Mycostatic	Fungistatic.
Mycotic	Relating to a mycosis or to a fungus.

Nail

Unguis.
Ingrown Nail – Ingrowing nail; ony-chocryptosis; a toenail, one edge of which is overgrown by the nailfold, possibly producing a pyogenic granuloma.

Necrobiosis

The physiologic or normal death of cells or tissues as a result of changes associated with development, aging, or use.

Necrobiotic

Pertaining to or characterized by necrobiosis.

Necrosis

The pathologic death of one or more cells, or of a portion of tissue or organ, resulting from irreversible damage.

Necrotic

Affected by or pertaining to necrosis.

Nerve

One or more bundles of fibers, forming part of a system which conveys impulses of sensation, motion, etc., between the brain or spinal cord and other parts of the body.

Neural

Relating to any structure that is composed of nerve cells or their processes, or that on further development will give rise to nerve cells.

Neuralgia

Neurodynia; nerve pain; pain of a severe, throbbing, or stabbing character in the course of distribution of a nerve.

Neurectomy	Neuroectomy; the excision of a part or segment of a nerve.
Neuritis	Inflammation of a nerve.
Neuroma	A tumor formed of nervous tissue.
Neuropathy	A disease of the nervous system.
Neurovascular	Relating to both nervous and vascular systems; relating to the nerves supplying the walls of the blood vessels.
Neutral position	That point at which a normal foot is neither inverted nor everted from the floor during stance.
Nosocomial	Relating to a hospital.
Nummular	Coined - shaped.

- O -

Oblique	Slanting, deviating from the perpendicular or the horizontal.
Onychalgia	Pain in the nails.
Onychatrophia	Atrophy of the nails.
Onychatrophy	Atrophy of the nails.
Onychauxis	A marked overgrowth of toenails.
Onychectomy	The removal of a toenail.

Onychia	Onychitis: onyxitis; inflammation of the matrix of the nail. When occurring on the lateral or medial border, it is called paronychia.
Onycho-Onych	Combing forms denoting nail.
Onychoclasis	Breaking of the nails.
Onychocryptosis	Ingrown nail.
Onychodystrophy	Dystrophic changes in the toenails occurring as a congenital defect or due to any illness or injury that may cause a malformed nail.
Onychogryphosis, Onychogryposis	An enlargement with increased thickening and curvature of the toenails.
Onycholysis	Loosening of the toenail.
Onychoma	A tumor arising from the nail bed.
Onychomadesis	The complete shedding of toenail usually associated with a systemic illness.
Onychomalacia	Abnormal softness of the toenails.
Onychomycosis	An involvement of a fungus infection of the toenails.
Onychopathic	Suffering from or relating to any disease of the toenails.
Onychophosis	A growth of horny epithelium in the nail bed.

Onychoplasty	Surgery on the nail matrix.
Onychoptosis	Falling off of the toenails.
Onychorrhexis	The abnormal brittleness of the toenails with splitting of the free edge.
Onychoschizia	The splitting of the toenails, in layers.
Operate	To work upon the foot by means of cutting or other instruments in order to perform surgery.
Operation	Any surgical procedure.
Orthotic	A device of varying design and construction that is applied externally to the foot, within the shoe, to restrict or facilitate motion, provide stability during locomotion, reduce or redistribute weight bearing forces and enhance total foot function.
Oscillometer	An apparatus or instrument used for measuring oscillations of the blood stream.
Oscillometric	Relating to the oscillometer readings or the records made by its use.
Osseous	Bony.
Osteo	Combining forms denoting bone.
Osteoarthritis	Degenerative or hypertrophic arthritis; degenerative joint disease; degeneration of articular cartilage.

Osteomyelitis	Inflammation of the bone marrow and adjacent bone.
Osteonecrosis	The death of bone.
Osteoporosis	The reduction in the quantity of bone or atrophy of skeletal tissue.
Osteoporotic	Pertaining to, characterized by, or causing a porous condition of the bones.
Osteotome	An instrument for the use in cutting bone.
Osteotomy	The cutting of bone, usually by means of a saw or chisel, for any purpose.

– P –

Pain	An unpleasant sensory and emotional experience associated with, or described in terms of, actual or potential tissue damage.
Palliate	A reduction of a condition; to relieve temporarily.
Palliative	The relief of symptoms without curing the underlying problem.
Palpate	To examine by the use of touch and pressure of the hands.
Palpation	The examination by means of the hands.

Pathogen	Any microorganism, virus, or other substance which causes disease.
Patient	An individual who suffers from any disease or condition and is under treatment for it.
Periosteum	The thick fibrous membrane that covers the entire surface of a bone except its articular cartilage.
Periostitis	Inflammation of the periosteum.
Phalanges	Plural of phalanx.
Phalanx	Any bone which comprises the toes.
Phlebitis	Inflammation of a vein.
Phlebo–Phleb	Combing forms denoting vein.
Phlebothrombosis	Thrombosis, or clotting, in a vein without primary inflammation.
Plantar	Relating to the bottom (sole) of the foot.
Plasty	A suffix which means molding or shaping or the result thereof, as in a surgical procedure.
Pod–, Podo	Combining forms meaning foot or foot–shaped.
Podagra	Gout, especially typical gout in the great toe.
Podiatrist	A practitioner of podiatry.

Podiatry	The specialty concerned with the diagnosis and/or medical, surgical, mechanical, physical and the treatment of the diseases, injuries and defects of the human foot.
Porokeratosis	A rare dermatosis in which there is a thickening of the stratum corneum and progressive centrifugal atrophy.
Post	A prefix which denotes after, behind or posterior.
Premedication	The administration of drugs prior to anesthesia.
Preoperative	Before surgery.
Preparation	To get ready.
Prescribe	The directions given a patient, either orally or in writing, for the preparation and administration of a preparation to be used in a treatment.
Prescription	The written formula for the preparation and administration of any remedy.
Pronation	The eversion and abduction of foot, causing a lowering of the medial edge.
Prophylaxis	The prevention of a condition or disease.
Prothesis	A fabricated substitute for a diseased or missing part of a foot.
Pruritis	Itching.

Purulent	Containing, consisting of, or forming pus.
Pus	A fluid product of inflammation and/or infection.

– R –

Remission	The abatement or the lessening in severity of the symptoms of a disease.
Resect	To cut off.
Resection	To remove.
Resorption	In bone, the removal of osseous tissue.

– S –

Scar	Cicatrix: the fibrous tissue replacing normal tissues destroyed by surgery, injury or disease.
Sensation	A feeling.
Sensitive	The ability to perceive sensations.
Sensitivity	1. The state of being sensitive. 2. In a result from a culture of a microorganism, that which is sensitive to an antibiotic.

Septicemia	A systemic disease caused by the multiplication of microorganisms in the circulating blood.
Sequela	A morbid entity following as a consequence of a surgery, disease or condition.
Side effect	A result of drug or other therapy in addition to or in extension of the desired therapeutic effect.
Sign	Any abnormality indicative of disease, discoverable by the examiner at his examination of the patient.
Site	Place; location.
Spasm	An involuntary muscular contraction.
Splint	An appliance for the prevention of the movement of a joint or for the fixation of displaced or movable parts.
Sponge	An absorbable material, such as gauze or prepared cotton, used to absorb fluids.
Sprain	An injury to a ligament when the joint is carried through a range of motion greater than normal, but without dislocation or fracture.
Status	State; condition.
Strain	An injury to the foot, resulting from the overuse or improper use.

Subluxation	An incomplete luxation or dislocation; though a relationship is altered, contact between joint surfaces remains.
Sudeck's Atrophy	Postraumatic osteoporosis.
Superior	Situated above or directed upward; opposite of inferior.
Supination	The inversion and abduction of the foot, causing a lifting of the medial edge.
Suture	1. The act of uniting two surfaces by sewing. 2. The material with which two surfaces are kept in apposition.
Swelling	An enlargement.
Symptom	Any departure from the normal in function, appearance, or sensation experienced by the patient.
Symptomatic	Indicative or relating to symptoms of a condition.
Synovitis	Inflammation of a synovial membrane, especially that of a joint.
Syringe	An instrument used for injecting or withdrawing of fluids.

– T –

Tabes	Progressive wasting or emaciation.

Tabes Diabetica	Diabetic neuropathy, especially of the motor nerves of the lower extremities, marked by a muscular atrophy and a steppage gait.
Tabes Dorsalis	Locomotor ataxia.
Talar	Relating to the talus.
Talipes	Any deformity of the foot involving the talus.
Talo	Combining form denoting the talus.
Talus	The ankle bone.
Tender	Sensitive – painful on pressure or contact.
Tenderness	Painfulness to pressure or contact.
Tendo	Combining form denoting a tendon.
Tendon	A fibrous cord or band that connects a muscle to a bone or other structure.
Tendonitis	Inflammation of a tendon.
Tenosynovitis	Inflammation of a tendon and its enveloping sheath.
Tenotomy	The surgical division of a tendon.
Therapy	The treatment of a disease or condition by various methods and/or modalities.
Thrombo-Thromb	Combining forms denoting blood clot or relation thereto.

Thrombophlebitis	Venous inflammation with thrombus formation.
Thrombosis	The formation of presence of a thrombus; clotting within a blood vessel.
Tibia	Shin bone.
Toxic	Poisonous.
Trauma	An injury.
Treatment	The medical or surgical management of a patient.
Trophic	Resulting from interruption of nerve supply.
Tyloma	Callosity.

– U –

Ulcer	A lesion on the surface of the skin or a mucous surface, caused by superficial loss of tissue, usually with inflammation.
Ungual	Relating to a nail or the nails.
Unguis	Nail plate; nail.

– V –

Valgus	Turned outward.

Varus	Bent or twisted inward.
Vaso	Combining form denoting a blood vessel.
Vasoconstriction	Narrowing of the blood vessels.
Vasodilation	Dilation of the blood vessels.
Vein	A blood vessel which carries blood towards the heart.
Verruca	Wart.

– W –

Wart	Verruca

– X –

X–ray	Roentgen ray.

– Z –

Z–plasty	A plastic procedure to elongate a contracted tendon or scar.

CASES

CASES

FOOT MALPRACTICE AND STANDARDS OF CARE

The following cases are examples of podiatric malpractice. The names of doctors, patients, and locations have been changed for reasons of confidentiality.

Case 1

MLF is a 14 year old athletic boy who loved to play basketball, baseball, and other school wide sports. One day MLF developed an inflamed and obviously infected left great toenail.

With his mother, Mike sought out the services of Dr. Berlin, a noted local general surgeon. Although we speak in this book of "podiatric standards of care," these same standards apply to other practitioners outside of podiatric medicine/surgery (including M.D.s, osteopaths, physical therapists) who render any sort of foot care. The surgery or specific medical technique may vary from one discipline to another, however, local and specialty variance notwithstanding, there are still general principles or standards regarding foot care throughout the country.

Dr. Berlin saw Mike on three separate occasions at his office, at which time he merely prescribed antibiotics for the infection. On September 10, 1981 Mike was admitted to a hospital where, on an outpatient basis, Dr. Berlin performed a left total toenail avulsion (removal) with matrixectomy (total nail bed destruction).

Mike returned to Dr. Berlin's office for postoperative care three days after the operation. "When will my nail grow back?" Mike asked. Dr. Berlin at this time explained to Mike and his mother that his nail would not grow back since a matrixectomy involves the destruction of the nail bed from which the nail grows.

In the months that followed not only was Mike without a toenail but he was also developing constant, unremitting pain at the surgical site.

With a referral from his attorney, Mike presented himself with his mother to our office for an evaluation of his case. Several questions arise as to the treatment Dr. Berlin rendered to Mike:

1. Was a culture and sensitivity test performed by Dr. Berlin on the patient?

2. Were Mike and his mother given an explanation as to the treatment he was about to receive and the possible risks and complications arising from a total nail avulsion with matrixectomy?

3. Did Dr. Berlin adhere to the standard of foot-medical/surgical care in treating a patient with an inflamed and infected toenail?

The answers to these questions:

1. It is considered standard foot-medical care to perform a culture and sensitivity test (C & S) on an infected toenail, or any infected body part, for that matter. The results of such a test allow the doctor to prescribe the antibiotic(s) most likely to succeed in eliminating the microorganisms responsible for the infection. Dr. Berlin did not perform a C & S on the patient. He prescribed antibiotics not knowing if his antibiotic would be effective against the microorganisms causing the infection. (See C & S section in laboratory medicine).

2. It is considered standard medical practice (in podiatry as well as in other branches of medi-

cine) to explain prior to any treatment plan, particularly in the case of surgery:

a) What the surgery involves.
b) Possible risks and complications.

The patient's mother signed a "consent for operation" form which listed the surgery as an "excision ingrown toenail, left great toenail." There was never a mention made, either verbally or in writing, of the matrixectomy (nail bed destruction). (See informed consent section).

3. In the case of an inflamed/infected toenail, it is accepted medical/surgical practice to first determine the microbiologic causative agent of the infection. Once this determination is made, the correct antibiotic should be prescribed. Removal of the offending nail border is indicated at this time. After the nail border removal is complete, soaks and antibiotics may be continued.

Dr. Berlin did not adhere to this standard. He proceeded to perform a nail removal and a matrixectomy without first following a more conservative path.

Dr. Berlin committed malpractice in the following instances:

1. He failed to perform a culture and sensitivity test. There is no way of knowing if the antibiotics he prescribed at the beginning of this treatment were effective against the infection.

2. Dr. Berlin failed to inform the patient and his guardian mother of the risks and complications of this particular surgery. As it turned out, the patient had a subungual exostosis (a protrusion of bone on the tip of the toe) which the nail serves to protect. By no longer having a nail on top of the toe, the patient now experiences al-

most constant pain to this area and can no longer participate in his high school sports.

3. Dr. Berlin failed to follow a more conservative plan of action namely, to proceed with one or more C & S, prescribe antibiotics and soaks. Also, preoperative x-rays were not taken to rule out a subungual exostosis which would be a relative contraindication to a nail matrixectomy.

Malpractice was committed by Dr. Berlin in at least three instances.

At the date of trial the doctor pleaded guilty to malpractice. The jury awarded the plaintiff $80,000 in damages for a wrongful toenail removal.

Case 2

Very often a seemingly minor and routine podiatric procedure can lead to devastating and unfortunate results. This is particularly true when commonly accepted procedure and standard precautions are not observed.

Consider the case of M.W., a 55 year old black male residing in a large metropolitan center. The patient is a diabetic of long standing, who in his earlier years was a weight lifter.

Since 1978 M.W. was being treated by his podiatrist, Dr. T. for the cutting of thick, horny nails and routine foot care.

In the summer of 1981, M.W. returned from his vacation with an inflamed, infected ingrown toenail right foot, medial border. The nail was embedded in the flesh and there was definite paronychia (that is, inflammation with pus about the margin of the nail). In an effort to relieve some of the pain, M.W. had cut out a hole in his sneaker,

140

but he continued with his recreational weight lifting and employment as a store clerk.

When M.W. presents himself to Dr. T. for treatment of his ingrown toenail, Dr. T. proceeds in the following manner:

1. The doctor cuts out a portion of the nail after giving a local anesthesia.

2. A topical antibiotic is applied to the area.

3. The toe is covered with a band-aid.

4. The patient is instructed to soak his toe two or three times daily for ten minute periods in luke-warm water.

5. The patient is instructed to apply neosporin powder (given as an Rx. by the doctor) after soaking and to keep the toe covered at all times except when soaking.

6. The patient is to return for his next office visit 2 weeks later.

M.W. returns for his scheduled appointment two weeks later. At this time the toe has become necrotic. There is now dead tissue and a yellow exudate (fluid) around the toenail. At the site of the nail avulsion procedure performed two weeks ago there are now pregangrenous changes evident in an area about 2 cm. in diameter.

Dr. T. proceeds to debribe with his scalpel and tissue nippers some of the necrotic tissue. The patient tells the doctor at this visit that the pain is the same as during the first visit; that is, constant unremitting. Dr. T instructs the patient to continue with his soaking twice daily.

A few days after this second office visit, M.W. calls Dr. T. to tell him the pain is still present and just as bad. M.W. states he cannot sleep properly at night because of the pain.

One week after the phone conversation, M.W. returns during his appointed time. There is now obvious dead tissue at the toe and gangrene has set in. At this point, Dr. T. refers the patient to an orthopedic surgeon.

On the same day as his office visit (two days after seeing Dr. T.) the orthopod hospitalizes M.W. The admitting diagnosis:

Diabetes mellitus.

Cellulitis/gangrene of the right great toe.

Vascular insufficiency.

The patient is in the hospital for two months, during which time the following procedures are performed:

1. A C & S (culture and sensitivity) of the gangrenous right toe.

2. Keflex IV drip is started pending the results of the C & S.

3. Two days after admission, an I & D (incision and drainage) of the toe is performed.

A day after the hospitalization, a vascular surgeon is called in to evaluate M.W.. He decides to perform an angiogram, the results of which lead him to perform a lumbar sympathectomy (that is, the surgical excision of a portion of the sympathetic nervous system). The purpose of the sympathectomy is to produce vasodilation and thereby improve circulation to the lower extremity and promote healing to the toe. Unfortunately, the sympathectomy is unsuccessful.

In the course of his examination of the patient, the orthopedic surgeon performs a venous filling test, which shows inadequacy. The feet are clinically cold. The dorsalis pedis, posterior tibial, and popliteal arteries are non-palpable. The patient complains of cold extremities and parasthesias. The sympathectomy is performed five days after admission. Eight days after admission the great toe is amputated at the metatarsophalangeal joint under general anesthesia.

Twelve days into the hospital stay, a venous graft is placed at Hunter's canal. The venous autograft is done, but unfortunately is not successful.

The gangrene continues to spread. Three weeks into the hospitalization an amputation is performed at the mid-tarsal joint (Lisfranc amputation).

Four weeks into the hospitalization, a B.K. (below knee) amputation is performed. The gangrene had spread further. After two months the patient is fitted with a stump. The patient brings suit against the podiatrist and the case is tried in court.

The Areas of Deviation: The basis of podiatric malpractice.

The podiatrist deviated from accepted podiatric practice in a number of instances:

    1. No Lower extremity (L.E.) exam was ever performed. No physical exam was taken of vascular and neurologic status of M.W. There was an inadequate history on the patient's medical status, medication and followup of his diabetes. There was no baseline studies, not even in 1978, when the patient first began treatment with Dr. T.

2. There was no physical exam taken for the current chief complaint (ingrown toenail).

3. No culture and sensitivity (C & S) was taken at any time.

4. No prophylactic antibiotic was given; no broad spectrum antibiotic, as called for in this situation of an apparent, fulminant infection.

5. No x-rays were taken.

6. The podiatrist never checked with the physician on the patient's status.

7. The intervals between appointments were too long. In the case of infection, particularly in the case of a diabetic with an infection where the consequences can be so devastating, as we have seen, followup visits should have been scheduled every 3 days.

8. Blood tests and urine tests should have been ordered to monitor the patient's diabetes.

In addition to all of the foregoing errors of omission, the patient should have been hospitalized when he came, at the first visit, at which time the following measures should have been instituted:

1. Bed rest.

2. Elevation of the limb.

3. IV antibiotics.

4. Surgical debridement.

5. Constant care.

The case was settled for $500,000 on the day trial was to begin.

Case 3

A 35 year old white male, E.K. resides in a large metropolitan area. E.K. works as a security guard in a high rise condominium.

One Sunday, while playing with his daughter, E.K. steps on a pin. He is rushed by ambulance to the hospital E.R., where he is seen by Dr. M.T., a first year podiatry resident.

Dr. M.T. orders x-rays to be taken. He scrubs the foot in an E.R. room and surgically explores for the needle. After one-half hour of effort, he succeeds in removing only 1/2 of the needle. The pin has entered the foot between the first and second toe of the right foot, approximately 3/4 inch from the front of the foot.

During his exploratory fishing, the doctor makes incisions both dorsally and plantarly (top and bottom).

The patient is given a sterile dressing to cover the foot. He is also given a postoperative, wooden-soled shoe, and told to report to the E.R. in 3 weeks.

The patient returns to the E.R. on the appointed day in a great deal of pain. The resident takes another set of x-rays. Once more he explores for the pin, using a plantar and dorsal approach. Once more Dr. M.T. is unsuccessful.

The resident tells the patient: "You're going to have to live with this problem. I have shrapnel from Vietnam, so you should be able to live with a pin in your foot."

Upon hearing this, the patient immediately seeks out

a private physician, an orthopedic surgeon.

The orthopedic surgeon begins with injection therapy and physical therapy to rest the foot and afford some temporary relief. After 11 months of continuous physical therapy the patient is hospitalized for the surgical removal of a foreign body.

The doctor takes grid x-rays to determine the precise location of the foreign body. In the O.R. itself, the doctor takes further x-rays using surgical pins as markers to locate the offending pin. He makes one dorsal incision and removes the remaining 1/2 of the pin from E.K.'s foot.

Almost one year from the date of the accident, E.K. is now free of the pin. However, he has sustained nerve damage and massive fibrosis because of the two prior operative procedures he underwent by Dr. M.T.

Even though the pin is removed, the patient still has a great deal of pain.

In spite of the pain, the patient must continue working on his feet and walking about in order to support his family. He is now unable to wear normal shoe gear. E.K. is now in almost constant pain. The quality of his life has diminished as a result of his injury and subsequent treatment.

Standards Of Care

The Areas of Deviation: The basis of podiatric malpractice.

1. The podiatry resident should have reported to his chief with this case since obviously it was a case

beyond his training and expertise. As it turned out during questioning, the resident had never had an opportunity to remove a deeply embedded foreign body from the foot.

2. The podiatrist should have performed the extrication procedure in an operating room (not an E.R. room) under sterile conditions.

3. Grid x-rays should have been taken. These are portable x-rays used to determine precise location of a foreign body.

4. The podiatrist's obligation to his patient in the case of a foreign body is to remove the material totally, and not to leave any remnant in the body.

5. In an obviously complicated case, such as this one, Dr. M.T. should have sought out assistance and have had at least one other assistant during the procedure. Better yet, he should have sought out the advice and assistance of a senior podiatrist or orthopedic surgeon experienced in foreign body removal.

A three day jury trial is held. The jury returns with a verdict against the doctor and hospital. It awards the plaintiff $305,000 in damages.

Case 4

This cases illustrates dramatically how important it is that the physician – surgeon not only be technically proficient and correct in his surgery, but also that he be fully knowledgeable about all medications he prescribes or administers to his patient, before surgery, during surgery, and after surgery. A technically perfect operation can be ruined and have disasterous consequences by the doctor's failure to be aware of contraindications and complications in the use of preoperative and postoperative medications.

A 26 year old "playboy bunny" presented one day to the podiatrist's office with a painful hammertoe of the third toe, left foot. The condition had been present for at least two years, was becoming increasingly more painful for the patient, who because of her work had to wear high heels all day long.

The doctor diagnosed the problem as "hammertoe deformity" of the third toe, left foot. Without doing any preoperative vascular study or preoperative blood workup, the podiatric surgeon performed an arthroplasty of the proximal interphalangeal joint using 6 cc. of 2% xylocaine **with epinephrine** as the local anesthetic.

The surgery went well and by all accounts seemed to follow accepted protocol of M.I.S. (minimal incision surgery). According to the doctor's surgical report the patient tolerated surgery well.

That night, despite the doctor's prescription of Dolobid (a nonnarcotic analgesic for moderate pain) the patient could not sleep. After the patient's distressed call, the doctor called the local pharmacy to prescribe over the phone a much stronger analgesic, namely, Demerol 50 mg., one tablet to be taken four times daily, or as needed.

The patient returned to the office the following day in excruciating pain.

After removing the postoperative bandages the doctor saw a toe which had undergone color changes to several shades of purple. The patient was complaining of having unbearable pain, despite her use of Demerol as prescribed.

Immediately upon examination the doctor knew what had gone wrong. He realized, too late, he was looking at the result of a vascular collapse to the toe brought about by the improper use of epinephrine (a local vasoconstrictor agent) which causes constriction, or narrowing of small blood vessels. The constriction was so great that tissue in the toe did not receive an adequate perfusion of blood, leading to ischemia, and ultimately, to tissue death.

The podiatrist referred his "playboy bunny" patient to a vascular surgeon, who immediately hospitalized the patient, whose toe was now turning shades of black.

The patient remained hospitalized for three weeks. The toe became necrotic, gangrenous and eventually had to be amputated at the metatarsal phalangeal joint, despite heroic efforts to save it.

The podiatrist made two crucial errors in this case:

1. He did not take a baseline vascular status on his patient. Although young and healthy, his 26 year old "bunny" had weak dorsalis pedis and posterior tibial artery pulses. Furthermore, many insurance companies now mandate that all preoperative patients undergo extensive vascular workup, which includes tests such as plethesmography, etc.

2. He injected a local anesthetic (lidocaine) mixed with a concentration of epinephrine (a potent vasoconstrictor), in which combination is contraindicated for digital (toe) anesthesia.

The "playboy bunny" can no longer wear open toe shoes. Furthermore, the patient is psychologically marred since her success in her modeling, acting career is dependent on her looks, which have been adversely affected following her toe amputation.

This case was settled prior to trial for $225,000.

Case 5

In this case, our patient, Mr. F.F., had a long term relationship with his podiatrist, one spanning almost 14 years.

During this course of time, Mr. F's circulatory status became progressively worse. In fact, during one visit in July 1979 Mr. F requested of Dr. O'Farrell that he be seen every three weeks instead of every four weeks because of his now constant, almost unremitting foot and leg pains.

Classically, patients who have compromised circulation to their extremities experience such pain.

Dr. O'Farrell did not see "the flying red flag." He performed an oscillimetric reading on the patient (to determine the rate of blood flow to the lower extremities) and obtained a reading of "O". At this point, based on his clinical finding and based on the patient's complaint, Dr. O'Farrell should have made a prompt referral to a vascular specialist. Mr. F was a walking time-bomb waiting to explode.

That explosion occurred October 27, 1979, when after a routine office visit the podiatrist burred a nail (standard practice) too vigorously and caused bleeding. Mr. F was admitted three weeks later with gangrene of the left great toe.

This gangrene eventually led to a foot and leg amputation over the course of several hospitalizations.

Three questions arise as to the care rendered Mr. F by Dr. O'Farrell:

    1. Why wasn't the patient referred to a vascular specialist after the office visit of July 13, 1979

when Dr. O'Farrell made a determination of "O" oscillometry reading?

2. Why wasn't the patient either referred to a vascular specialist or hospitalized on October 27, 1979 when the podiatrist burred the nail too deeply and caused bleeding?

3. Is there a causal relationship between Dr. O'Farrell's care and treatment and the patient's ensueing amputation?

The answers to the aforementioned questions:

1. With an oscillometric reading of zero, given the patient's persistent complaints about foot/leg pains, and given the patient's current state of health, Dr. O'Farrell should have taken affirmative action and either referred Mr. F.F. to a vascular specialist or else hospitalized the patient immediately, where he could have recieved vascular workup and treatment.

2. When Dr. O'Farrell had lacerated the patient's foot, he was obligated to obtain an immediate emergency consultation by a vascular specialist or else hospitalize the patient for definitive care. With Mr. F.F.'s precarious vascular status Dr. O'Farrell should have been alert to a vascular breakdown and taken all the precautions he could have to prevent a disaster. He failed to do this.

3. There is certainly a direct causal relationship between Dr. O'Farrell's treatment and Mr. F.F.'s eventual loss of his left lower extremity.

Dr. O'Farrell knew from the patient's first visit on November 23, 1971 that the patient had a history of lower extremity circulation compromise. On July 13, 1979, the patient asked to be seen every three weeks instead of every four weeks because of his now almost unremitting extremity pains (a classic sign of ischemia or vascular shutdown). The request to be seen more frequently should have been a "red flag" to Dr. O'Farrell. The zero oscillometric reading obtained a few weeks later at his office should have been the final signal.

All the foregoing signs and symptoms are indicative of peripheral vascular shutdown and failure. Had Dr. O'Farrell referred Mr. F.F. to a vascular specialist at an earlier date, as early as September 1979, the patient would not have required an amputation of the left toe, then foot, then entire leg, at this time.

Dr. O'Farrell failed to recognize the red flags. His mistake was a failure to make a referral to another specialist in a timely fashion. The cost to him and his insurance carrier $225,000. The cost to Mr. F.F., the loss of a limb.

Case 6

This is the story of Mr. T. Bird, a 53 year old white male, industrial researcher at a major manufacturing firm. Mr. T. Bird consulted Dr. Faust for a painful lesion underneath the third metatarsal head of the right foot. Dr. Faust recommeneded corrective surgery for the problem and Mr. T. Bird was eager to undergo this procedure to correct his longstanding painful foot ailment.

Dr. Faust performed surgery for the affected area. The surgery was a metaphyseal osteotomy, and then Dr. Faust went on to perform a "tenotomy and capsulotomy" near the surgical site.

Unfortunately for Mr. T. Bird (and later for Dr. Faust), the tenotomy and capsulotomy resulted in a toe with diminished ability to dorsiflex (bend upwards). The absence of dorsiflexion in the toe caused Mr. T. Bird pain

152

and difficulty in walking.

The unfortunate result of the surgery was compounded by the doctor's failure to inform the patient prior to surgery as to the precise procedure(s) the surgeon was about to undertake. The podiatric surgeon performed an operation on an area about which Mr. T. Bird was unaware prior to surgery and to which Mr. T. Bird had never given consent, either verbally or in writing.

The doctor committed malpractice in this case by his failure to disclose a procedure he was to perform, and by his failure to obtain informed consent. The doctor obtained consent for the osteotomy, but not for the tenotomy and capsulotomy. The major risk associated with a tenotomy and capsulotomy is a toe with diminished dorsiflexion and resultant pain during ambulation.

Unfortunately the risk did occur and the problem was compounded by the fact that the doctor had failed to obtain consent for his tenotomy and capsulotomy procedure.

The jury awarded the plaintiff $15,000 for his poor toe function following surgery, and for the doctor's failure to obtain an informed consent.

The doctor who took the liberty of performing a procedure about which he did not inform his patient and for which he did not obtain consent opened up a "Pandora's Box" of problems for himself.

The failure to diagnose, but to treat properly, does not consitute malpractice when the desired effect or a resolution of the problem occurs. However, the failure to diagnose, coupled with the failure to treat properly, thereby causing harm or ill- effect to the patient, does constitute malpractice.

STATE CONCEPTS OR DEFINITIONS OF THE TERM PODIATRY

STATE CONCEPTS OR DEFINITIONS OF THE TERM PODIATRY

The American Podiatric Medical Association (A.P.M.A.) has furnished us with a listing of concepts/- scope of practice for podiatry, which is being reprinted here, in part, with permission, and with our thanks.

Alabama

". . . the diagnosis and treatment of the human foot and shall include the diagnosis and medical, surgical, mechanical, manipulative, or electrical treatment of any ailment of the human foot. Surgical treatment is the use of any cutting instrument to treat a disease, ailment or condition including the phalanges and metatarsals but not the tarsals." ". . . and using only local anesthetics."

Alaska

". . . medical, mechanical, and surgical treatment of ailments of the foot, the muscles and tendons of the leg governing the functions of the foot, and superficial lesions of the hand other than those associated with trauma, the use of preparations, medicines, and drugs as are necessary for the treatment of these ailments, the treatment of the local manifestations of systemic diseases as they appear in the hand and foot except that patient must be referred to physician or osteopath for treatment of the systemic diseases, general anesthetics may be used only in approved podiatry colleges and approved hospitals, and the use of X-ray or radium for therapeutic purposes is not permitted."

Arizona

". . . diagnosis, or medical, surgical, mechanical, man-ipulative, or electrical treatment of ailments of the human foot and leg but does not include amputation of the toe, foot, or leg, nor administration of an anesthetic other than local."

Arkansas

". . . diagnosis, medical, mechanical and surgical treatment of ailments of the human foot . . . no podiatrist shall amputate the human foot or toes or use any anesthe-tic other than local."

California

". . . the diagnosis, medical surgical, mechanical, man-ipulative, and electrical treatment of the human foot in-cluding the nonsurgical treatment of the muscles and ten-dons of the leg governing the functions of the foot. No podiatrists shall do any amputation or administer an anesthetic other than local."

Colorado

". . . the diagnosis and medical, surgical, mechanical, manipulative, and electrical treatment of ailments of the human toe, foot, and leg, excepting any amputation and excepting the administration of an anesthetic other than local".

Connecticut

". . . the diagnosis, prevention and treatment of foot ailments including the prescription, administering and dispensing of drugs and controlled substances in schedules II, III, IV or V, in accordance with subsection (d) of section 19-460, in connection therewith, practice of surgery upon the feet provided if an anesthetic other than a local anesthetic is required, such surgery shall be performed in a general hospital accredited by the Joint Commission on Accreditation of Hospitals by a licensed podiatrist who is accredited by such hospitals, dressing, padding and strapping of the feet making of models of the feet and the palliative and mechanical treatment of functional structural ailments of the feet, not including the amputation of the leg, foot or toes or the treatment of systemic diseases other than local manifestations in the foot."

Delaware

". . . the diagnosis and the medical, surgical, mechanical, manipulative and electrical treatment of all ailments of the human foot and leg, excepting amputation of the foot or leg or the administration of an anesthetic other than local".

District Of Columbia

". . . the surgical, medical, or mechanical treatment of any ailment of the human foot, except the amputation of the foot or any of the toes, and, also except the use of an anesthetic other than a local one".

Florida

". . . diagnosis and medical, surgical, palliative, and mechanical treatment of ailments of the human foot and leg. The surgical treatment of ailments of the human foot and leg shall be limited anatomically to that part below the anterior tibial tubercle. The practice of podiatry shall include the amputation of the toes or other parts of the foot but shall not include the amputation of the foot or leg in its entirety. A podiatrist may prescribe drugs that relate specifically to the scope of practice authorized herein".

Georgia

". . . diagnosis, medical, surgical, mechanical, manipulative and electrical treatment limited to the ailments of the human foot and leg. No podiatrist shall do any amputation or use any anesthetic other than local".

Hawaii

". . . medical, surgical, mechanical, manipulative, and electrical diagnosis and treatment of the human foot, including the nonsurgical treatment of the muscles and tendons of the leg governing the functions of the foot, but does not include any amputation, treatment of systemic conditions or the use of any anesthetic except local anesthetic".

Idaho

". . . diagnosis and mechanical, electrical, medical, physical and surgical treatment of ailments of the human foot and leg and the casting of feet for the purpose of preparing or prescribing corrective appliances, prosthetics, and/or the making of custom shoes for corrective treatment provided, however, that the casting of feet for preparing corrective appliances, prosthetics and/or custom shoes may be permitted on the prescription of a duly licensed person in the healing arts in this state. Podiatrist shall be limited in their practice to the human foot and leg. Surgical treatment, as herein used shall be held to mean the surgical treatment of the foot, but shall not include the amputation of foot or leg, surgery of the leg, or use of any anesthetic other than local anesthetics, except that a podiatrist may administer narcotics and medications in the treatment of ailments of the human foot and leg in the same manner as a physician and surgeon. A podiatrist within the scope of this act is a physician and surgeon of the foot."

Illinois

". . . physician licensed to practice podiatric medicine, which involves the diagnosis and medical, physical or surgical treatment of the ailments of the human foot, with the exception that administration of general anesthetics or amputation of the foot shall not be included".

Indiana

". . . diagnosis, medical, surgical and mechanical treatment of ailments of the human foot. No podiatrist shall amputate the human foot or toe or toes, or use or administer any anesthetic other than local".

Iowa

". . . one who examines or diagnoses or treats ailments of the human foot, medically or surgically." ". . . shall not authorize the licensee to amputate the human foot or perform any surgery on the human body at or above the ankle or use any anesthetics other than local. A registered podiatrist may prescribe and administer drugs for the treatment of human foot ailments. . ."

Kansas

"A registered podiatrist shall be authorized to prescribe such drugs or medicines, and to perform such surgery on the human foot or toes as may be necessary to the proper practice of podiatry, but no podiatrist shall amputate the human foot or toes or administer any anesthetic other than local".

Kentucky

". . . profession of the health sciences which deals with the examination, diagnosis, treatment, and prevention of diseases, conditions, and malfunctions affecting the human foot and its related or governing structures, by employment of medical, surgical or other means." "Podiatrist is a physician and surgeon who has graduated from a college of podiatric medicine accredited by the Council on Podiatry Education of the American Podiatry Association or approved by state licensing boards."

Louisiana

". . . that profession of the health sciences which deals with the prevention, examination, diagnosis, medical, surgical and adjuvant treatment of the human foot. Surgical treatment of the foot involving use of general or spinal anesthesia must be performed in a hospital accredited by the JCAH. The administration of general or spinal anesthesia by a podiatrist is prohibited".

Maine

". . . diagnosis and treatment of the human foot by medical, mechanical, or surgical means without the use of anesthetic other than local."

Maryland

". . . diagnose or surgically, medically, or mechanically treat any ailment of the human foot." It does not include (I) arthrodesis of two or more tarsal bones, (II) complete Tarsal Osteotomy; or (III) administration of an anesthetic, other than a local anesthetic.

Massachusetts

". . . diagnosis and the treatment of the structure of the human foot by medical, mechanical, surgical, manipulative and electrical means without the use of other than local anesthetics, and excepting treatment of systemic conditions, and excluding amputations of the foot or toes."

Michigan

". . . physician and surgeon. . ." who performs the ". . . examination, diagnosis, and treatment of abnormal nails, superficial excrescences occurring on the human hands and feet, including corns, warts, callosities, and bunions and arch troubles or the treatment medically, surgically, mechanically or by physiotherapy of ailments of human feet or ankles as they affect the condition of the feet. It does not include amputation of human feet or the use or administration of anesthetics other than local".

Minnesota

". . . diagnosis or medical, mechanical, or surgical treatment of the ailments of the human hand or foot . . . shall include the fitting or recommending of appliances, devices or shoes for correction or relief of minor foot ailments except the amputation of the foot, toes, or fingers or the use of anesthetics other than local".

Mississippi

". . . the diagnosis and medical, mechanical, electrical, and surgical treatment of the ailments of the human foot, such as corns, calluses, warts, arches, ingrowing and abnormal nails, bunions, and similar conditions, and practitioners of podiatry, or chiropody, shall be allowed to use such mechanical appliances as may be deemed necessary for the relief of cure of such ailments of the feet, except amputation of the foot or toes, or the use of anesthetics other than local anesthetics related to the part affected used to prevent operative or mechanical pain, provided that massage of the leg in connection with such treatment is not prohibited.

Missouri

". . . the diagnosis, medical, physical, or surgical treatment of ailments of the human foot, with the exception of administration of general anesthetics, or amputation of the foot and with the further exception of surgery on children under the age of one year. Podiatrist is defined as a physician of the foot. The use of drugs and medicines in the treatment of the foot shall not include the treatment of systemic diseases".

Montana

". . . the diagnosis, medical, surgical, mechanical, manipulative and electrical treatment of ailments of the human foot. No podiatrist shall amputate the human foot or toes or administer or use anesthetics other than local".

Nebraska

". . . diagnosis, medical, physical, or surgical treatment of the ailments of the human foot, except (a) the amputation of the foot or toes; (b) the removal of all of any bone of the foot except the distal phalanges; (c) the general medical treatment of any systemic disease causing manifestations in the foot; and (d) the administration of anesthetics other than local".

Nevada

". . . the diagnosis and the medical, surgical, mechanical, manipulative, and electrical treatment of all ailments of the human foot and leg not in connection with the practice of another license profession, except amputation of the foot or leg or the administration of an anesthetic other than local".

New Hampshire

". . . legal authority to diagnose and to treat by

medical, mechanical, electrical, and surgical means, ailments of the human foot. Medical treatment includes the parenteral use of drugs in accordance with the podiatrist's drug license. Surgery can be performed by duly trained podiatrists up to the ankle, excluding amputations. Podiatrists cannot administer general anesthetic."

New Jersey

". . . diagnosis or treatment of, or the holding out of a right or ability to diagnose or treat, any ailment of the human foot, including local manifestations of systemic diseases as they appear on the lower leg or foot but not treatment of systemic diseases of any other part of the body, or the holding out of a right or ability to treat the same by any one or more of the following means, local medical, mechanical, surgical, manipulative and physiotherapeutic, including the application of any of the aforementioned means to the lower leg and ankle for the treatment of a foot ailment. Such means shall not be construed to include the amputation of the leg or foot. The term "local medical" herein before mentioned shall be construed to mean the prescription or use of a therapeutic agent or remedy where the action or reaction is intended for a localized area or part."

Annotation concerning the amendment to the law of 1977 45; 5-7

"The Senate Institutions, Health and Welfare Committee statement to Senate Bill No. 720 – Laws of 1977, c. 83 Purpose of the Bill to remove certain restrictions on the diagnostic and treatment activities of licensed podiatrists. The New Jersey Senate expressed its intent to amend the statute governing the practice of podiatry to permit podiatrists to: (1) perform all kinds of surgery of the foot, not just "minor" surgery; (2) treat the lower leg and ankle when necessary for the cure of a foot ailment; (3) treat tuberculosis, osteomyelitis, malignancies, syphilis and diabetes where these diseases manifest themselves on the lower leg or foot; and (4) treat the rear foot as well as the forefoot."

"The means of treatment employed by podiatrists may not be construed to include amputation of the leg or foot under the provisions of the Bill." "The Committee amended the Bill to remove any suspicion that podiatrists might now be permitted to treat systemic diseases of parts of the body other than the lower leg or foot. This amendment was proposed by the State Board of Medical Examiners."

New Mexico

". . . engaging in that primary health care profession, members of which examine, diagnose, treat and prevent by medical, surgical and mechanical means ailments affecting the human foot and ankle, and the structures governing their functions, but does not include amputation of the foot or the personal administration of a general anesthetic. A podiatrist, under the laws of this state, is defined as a foot or podiatric physician."

New York

". . . diagnosing, treating, operating and prescribing for any disease, injury, deformity or other condition of the foot or operating on the bones, muscles or tendons of the feet for the correction of minor deficiencies and deformities of a mechanical and functional nature." It "includes treating simple and uncomplicated fractures of the bones of the foot, administering only local anesthetics for therapeutic purposes as well as for anesthesia, treating under general anesthesia administered by authorized persons, using nonnarcotic postoperative sedatives, but not treating any part of the human body nor treating fractures of the malleoli or cutting operations upon the malleoli. A podiatrist . . . after certification by the education department of the State of New York, in accordance with qualifications established by the commissioner, shall have the right to administer or prescribe narcotics."

North Carolina

". . . the surgical or medical or mechanical treatment of all ailments of the human foot, except the amputation of the foot or toes or the administration of an anesthetic other than local and except the correction of clubfoot deformity and triple arthrodesis."

North Dakota

". . . one who examines, diagnoses, and treats ailments of the human foot by medical, surgical, and other means, except amputation of the foot that can be done with or without a local anesthetic."

Ohio

". . . medical, mechanical, and surgical treatment of ailments of the foot, the muscles and tendons of the leg governing the functions of the foot, and superficial lesions of the hand other than those associated with trauma. Podiatrists are permitted the use of such preparations, medicines, and drugs as may be necessary for the treatment of such ailments. The podiatrist may treat the local manifestations of systemic disease itself. General anesthetics may be used under this section only in colleges of podiatry approved by the medical board and in hospitals approved by the Joint Commission on Accreditation of Hospitals or the American Osteopathic Association. The use of X- ray or radium for therapeutic purposes is not permitted. Certified podiatrists are authorized to use the title "physician" or "surgeon".

Oklahoma

". . . in any way examining, diagnosing, recommending for prescribing for, caring for or treating in this State, ailments, diseased conditions, deformities or injuries of the human foot (except amputation of the foot), whether or not done directly thereon. A podiatrist may also diagnose, recommend, prescribe, fit, build or furnish pads, inserts, appliances, casts and may use anesthetics, medications, in connection with examining and diagnosing foot ailments."

Oregon

". . . diagnosis or the medical, physical or surgical treatment of ailments of the human foot, except treatment involving the use of a general or spinal anesthetic unless the treatment is performed in a hospital certified in the manner described in ORS 441.055 (2) and is under the supervision of or in collaboration with a physician licensed to practice medicine by the board of Medical Examiners for the State of Oregon. "Podiatry" does not include the administration of general or spinal anesthetics or the amputation of the foot."

Pennsylvania

". . . shall mean the diagnosis and treatment including mechanical and surgical treatment of ailments of the foot, and those anatomical structures of the leg governing the functions of the foot and the administration and prescription of drugs incidental thereto. It shall include treatment of local manifestations of systemic diseases as they appear on the foot but not include amputation of the leg or foot or treatment of systemic diseases of any other part of the body."

Puerto Rico

". . . the diagnosis of foot ailments, the dressing, padding and strapping of the foot, the making of plaster models of the feet and the palliative, medical, surgical, manipulative, electrical and mechanical treatment of continual disturbances of the feet, not including the amputation of the foot or the use of anesthetics other than local."

Rhode Island

". . . the diagnosis of foot ailments, the dressing, padding and strapping of the feet, the making of plaster models of the feet and the palliative, medical, surgical, manipulative, electrical and mechanical treatment of functional disturbances of the feet, not including the amputation of the foot or the use of anesthetics other than local."

South Carolina

". . . the diagnosis, medical and surgical treatment limited to ailments of the human foot, except the administration of an anesthetic other than local."

South Dakota

". . . the medical, mechanical, and surgical treatment of the human foot. A podiatrist shall not be authorized to amputate the human foot, a toe or toes, or remove all or any bone other than those bones in the toes, or perform any surgery on the human body at or above the ankle, or administer anesthetics other than local anesthetics."

Tennessee

". . . examines, diagnoses, or treats medically, mechanically, or surgically the ailments of the human foot, including the use and prescribing of drugs and medications but excluding the direct application of general anesthesia by a podiatrist and the amputation of the foot."

Texas

". . . treatment or offer to treat any disease or disorder, physical injury or deformity, or ailment of the human foot by any system or method."

Utah

". . . who examines, diagnoses or treats, medically, mechanically, or surgically, the ailments of the human foot or massages in connection therewith, but nothing in this chapter shall be construed to permit the use of anesthetics other than local, or the amputation of the toes or foot."

Vermont

". . . the medical, mechanical, surgical, electrical, manipulation, strapping and bandaging treatment of the ailments pertaining to the human foot, not requiring amputation of the foot or toes or the use of anesthetics other than local."

Virginia

". . . the medical, mechanical, and surgical treatment of the ailments of the human foot, but does not include amputation of the foot or toes. Podiatrists shall not perform surgery on patients under a general anesthetic except in a hospital approved by the Joint Commission on Accreditation of Hospitals and shall perform such surgery only to the extent permitted by rules and regulations of such hospital."

Washington

". . . diagnosis and the medical, surgical, mechanical, manipulative, and electrical treatments of ailments of the human foot. A podiatrist is a podiatric physician and surgeon of the foot licensed to treat ailments of the foot, except for: (1) amputation of the foot; and (2) administration of a spinal anesthetic or any anesthetic which renders the patient unconscious, or the administration and prescription of drugs including narcotics, other than required to perform the services authorized for the treatment of the feet, and (3) treatment of systemic conditions."

West Virginia

". . . the examination, diagnosis, treatment, prevention and care of conditions and functions of the human foot by medical, surgical and other scientific knowledge and methods, and medical and surgical treatment of warts and other dermatological lesions of the hand which similarly occur in the foot. When a podiatrist uses other than local anesthesia, in the surgical treatment of the foot, such anesthesia must be administered by or under the direction of an anesthesiologist or certified nurse anesthetist authorized under the state of West Virginia to administer anesthesia. A medical evaluation shall be made by a physician of every patient prior to the administration of other than local anesthesia."

Wisconsin

". . . the diagnosis or mechanical, medical or surgical treatment, or treatment by the use of drugs, of the feet, but does not include amputations other than digits of the foot or the use of a general anesthetic unless administered by or under the direction of a person licensed to practice medicine and surgery. Diagnosis or treatment shall include no portion of the body above the feet except that diagnosis and treatment shall include the tendons and muscles of the lower leg insofar as they shall be involved in the conditions of the feet."

Wyoming

". . . the diagnosis or the medical, mechanical or surgical treatment of the ailments of the human foot but does not include the amputation of the foot or toes or the use of anesthetics other than local."

ILLUSTRATIONS OF FOOT ANATOMY

DORSAL-BONES

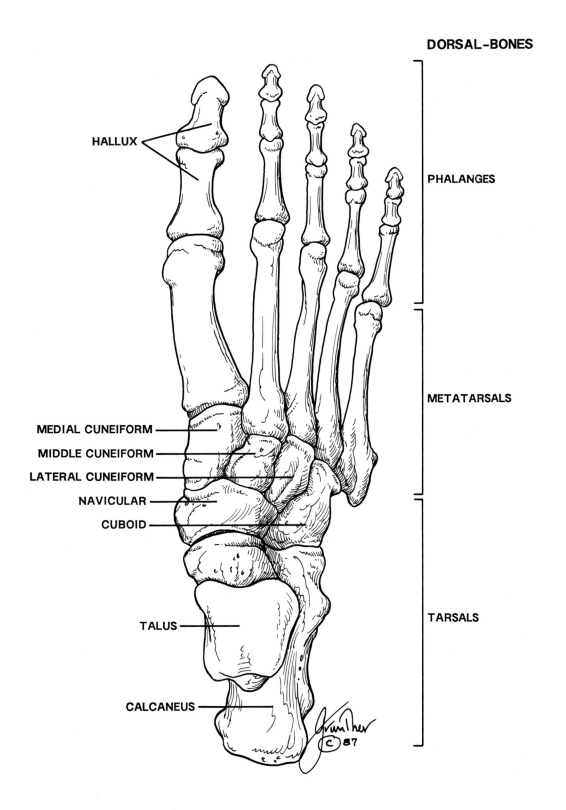

HALLUX

PHALANGES

MEDIAL CUNEIFORM

MIDDLE CUNEIFORM

LATERAL CUNEIFORM

METATARSALS

NAVICULAR

CUBOID

TALUS

TARSALS

CALCANEUS

PLANTAR-BONES

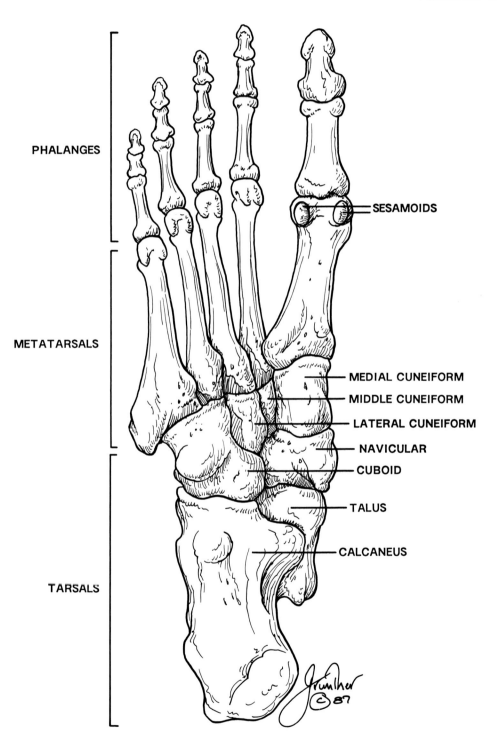

PHALANGES

SESAMOIDS

METATARSALS

MEDIAL CUNEIFORM

MIDDLE CUNEIFORM

LATERAL CUNEIFORM

NAVICULAR

CUBOID

TALUS

CALCANEUS

TARSALS

DORSAL-MUSCLES

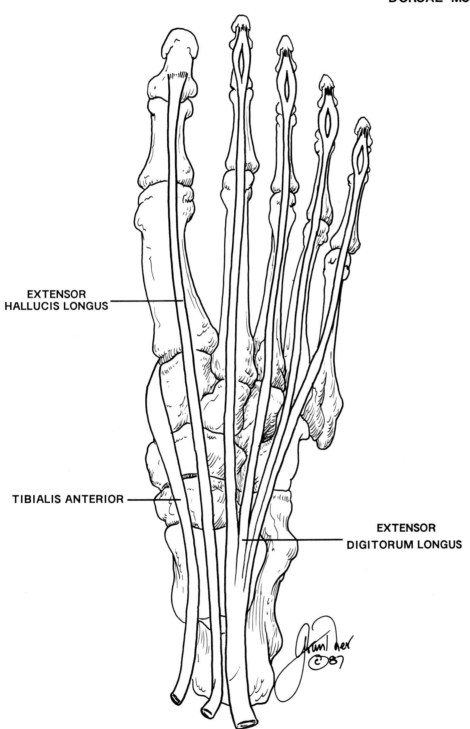

EXTENSOR
HALLUCIS LONGUS

TIBIALIS ANTERIOR

EXTENSOR
DIGITORUM LONGUS

DORSAL-MUSCLES

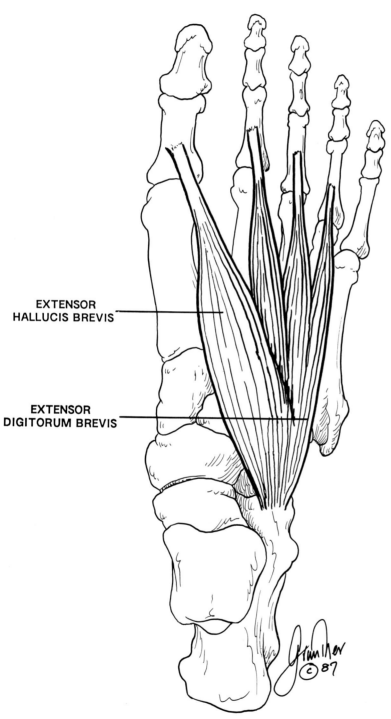

EXTENSOR
HALLUCIS BREVIS

EXTENSOR
DIGITORUM BREVIS

PLANTAR MUSCLES (1)

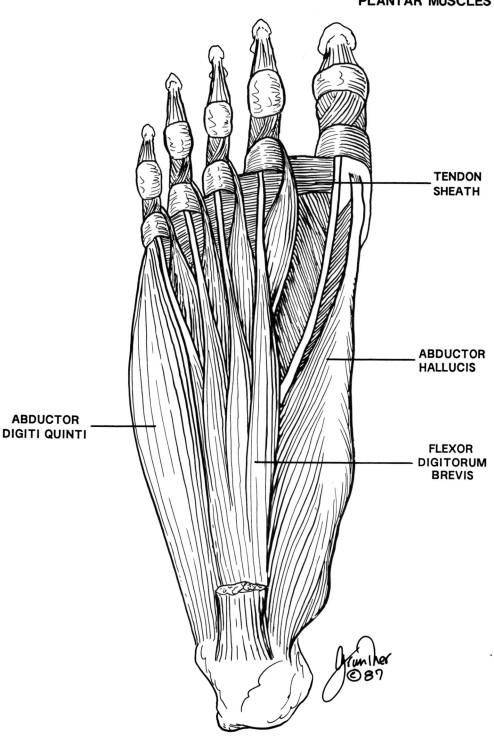

TENDON SHEATH

ABDUCTOR HALLUCIS

ABDUCTOR DIGITI QUINTI

FLEXOR DIGITORUM BREVIS

PLANTAR MUSCLES (2)

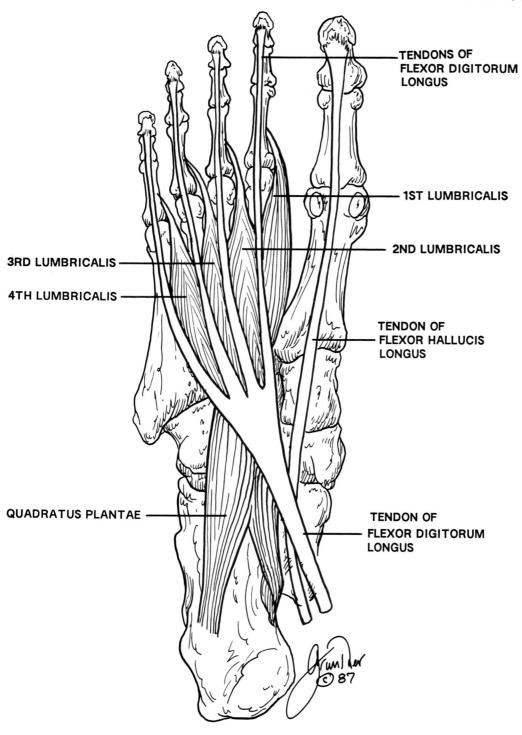

TENDONS OF
FLEXOR DIGITORUM
LONGUS

1ST LUMBRICALIS

2ND LUMBRICALIS

3RD LUMBRICALIS

4TH LUMBRICALIS

TENDON OF
FLEXOR HALLUCIS
LONGUS

QUADRATUS PLANTAE

TENDON OF
FLEXOR DIGITORUM
LONGUS

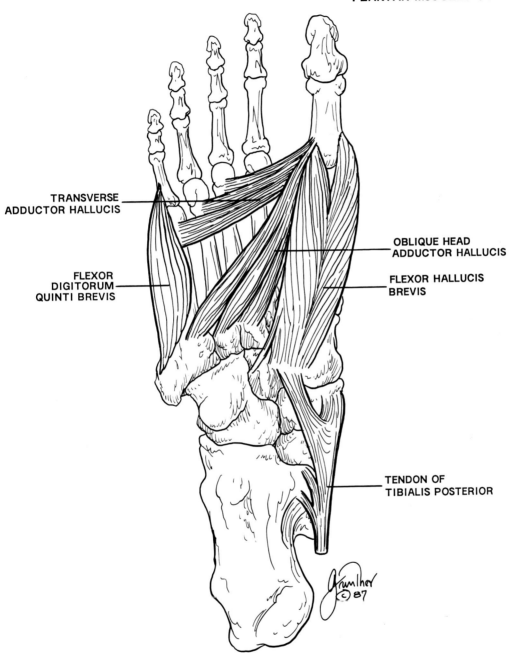

PLANTAR MUSCLES (3)

TRANSVERSE
ADDUCTOR HALLUCIS

OBLIQUE HEAD
ADDUCTOR HALLUCIS

FLEXOR
DIGITORUM
QUINTI BREVIS

FLEXOR HALLUCIS
BREVIS

TENDON OF
TIBIALIS POSTERIOR

PLANTAR MUSCLES (4)

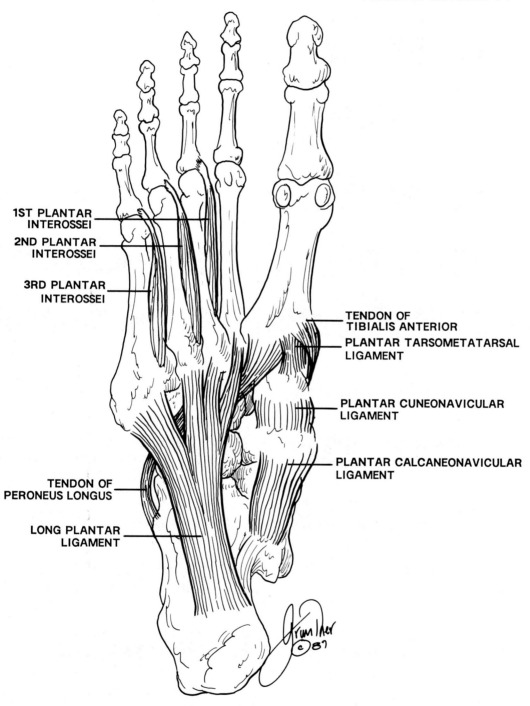

1ST PLANTAR
INTEROSSEI

2ND PLANTAR
INTEROSSEI

3RD PLANTAR
INTEROSSEI

TENDON OF
TIBIALIS ANTERIOR

PLANTAR TARSOMETATARSAL
LIGAMENT

PLANTAR CUNEONAVICULAR
LIGAMENT

PLANTAR CALCANEONAVICULAR
LIGAMENT

TENDON OF
PERONEUS LONGUS

LONG PLANTAR
LIGAMENT

DORSAL-ARTERIES

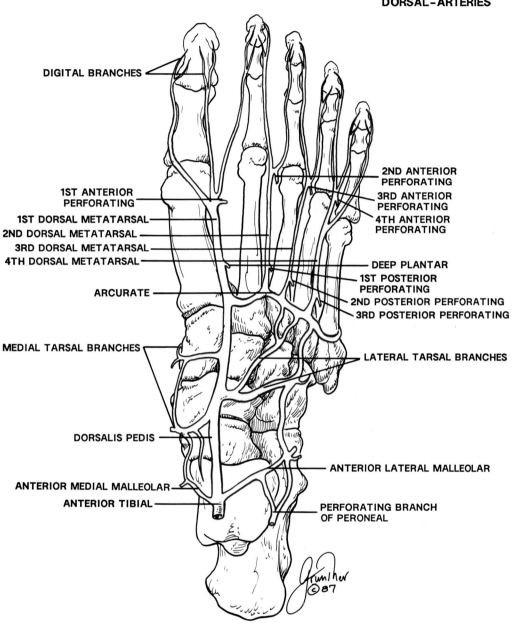

DIGITAL BRANCHES

2ND ANTERIOR PERFORATING

3RD ANTERIOR PERFORATING

4TH ANTERIOR PERFORATING

1ST ANTERIOR PERFORATING

1ST DORSAL METATARSAL

2ND DORSAL METATARSAL

3RD DORSAL METATARSAL

4TH DORSAL METATARSAL

DEEP PLANTAR

1ST POSTERIOR PERFORATING

2ND POSTERIOR PERFORATING

3RD POSTERIOR PERFORATING

ARCURATE

MEDIAL TARSAL BRANCHES

LATERAL TARSAL BRANCHES

DORSALIS PEDIS

ANTERIOR LATERAL MALLEOLAR

ANTERIOR MEDIAL MALLEOLAR

ANTERIOR TIBIAL

PERFORATING BRANCH OF PERONEAL

PLANTAR-ARTERIES

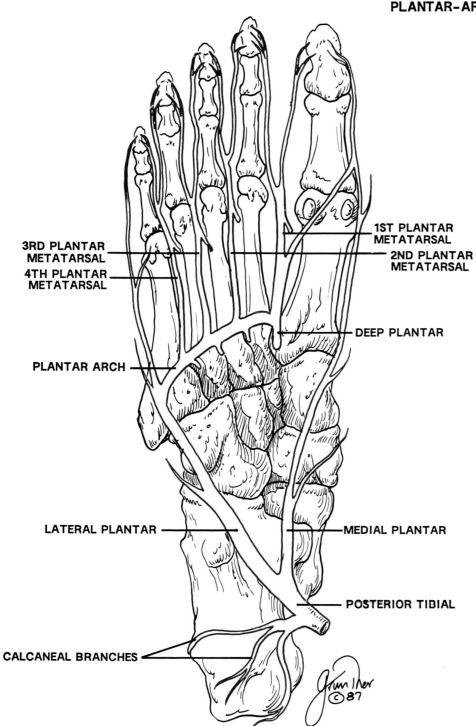

1ST PLANTAR
METATARSAL

3RD PLANTAR
METATARSAL

2ND PLANTAR
METATARSAL

4TH PLANTAR
METATARSAL

DEEP PLANTAR

PLANTAR ARCH

LATERAL PLANTAR

MEDIAL PLANTAR

POSTERIOR TIBIAL

CALCANEAL BRANCHES

DORSAL-VEINS

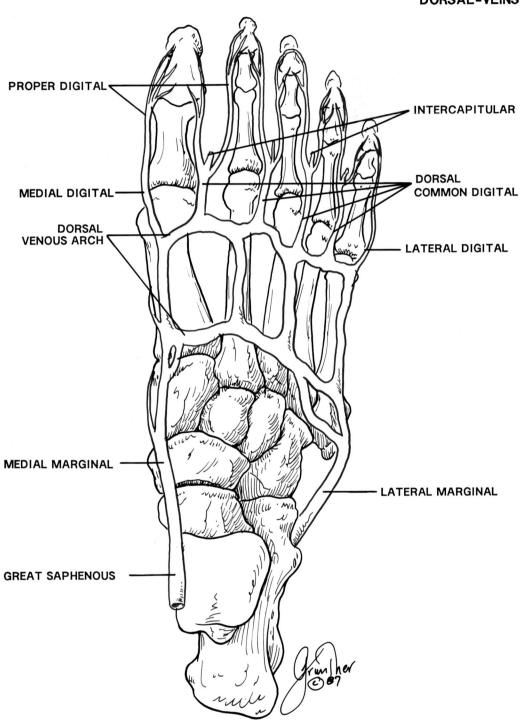

PROPER DIGITAL

INTERCAPITULAR

MEDIAL DIGITAL

DORSAL
COMMON DIGITAL

DORSAL
VENOUS ARCH

LATERAL DIGITAL

MEDIAL MARGINAL

LATERAL MARGINAL

GREAT SAPHENOUS

PLANTAR-VEINS

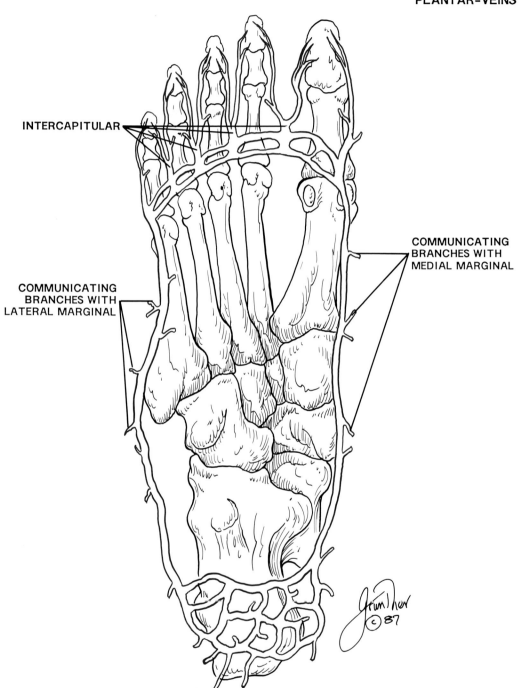

INTERCAPITULAR

COMMUNICATING
BRANCHES WITH
MEDIAL MARGINAL

COMMUNICATING
BRANCHES WITH
LATERAL MARGINAL

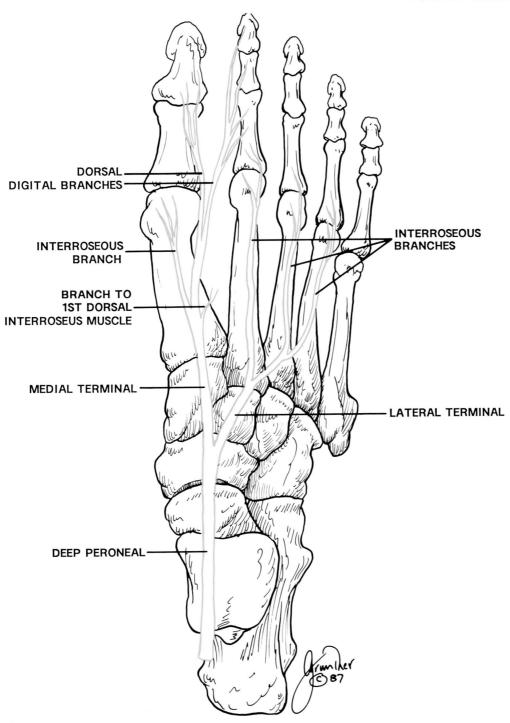

DORSAL NERVES

DORSAL
DIGITAL BRANCHES

INTERROSEOUS
BRANCH

BRANCH TO
1ST DORSAL
INTERROSEUS MUSCLE

MEDIAL TERMINAL

DEEP PERONEAL

INTERROSEOUS
BRANCHES

LATERAL TERMINAL

DORSAL-NERVES

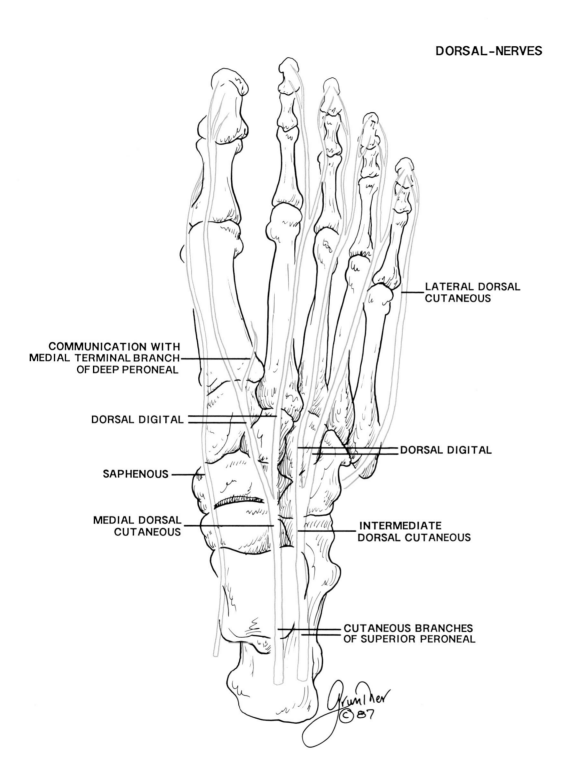

LATERAL DORSAL
CUTANEOUS

COMMUNICATION WITH
MEDIAL TERMINAL BRANCH
OF DEEP PERONEAL

DORSAL DIGITAL

DORSAL DIGITAL

SAPHENOUS

MEDIAL DORSAL
CUTANEOUS

INTERMEDIATE
DORSAL CUTANEOUS

CUTANEOUS BRANCHES
OF SUPERIOR PERONEAL

PLANTAR-NERVES

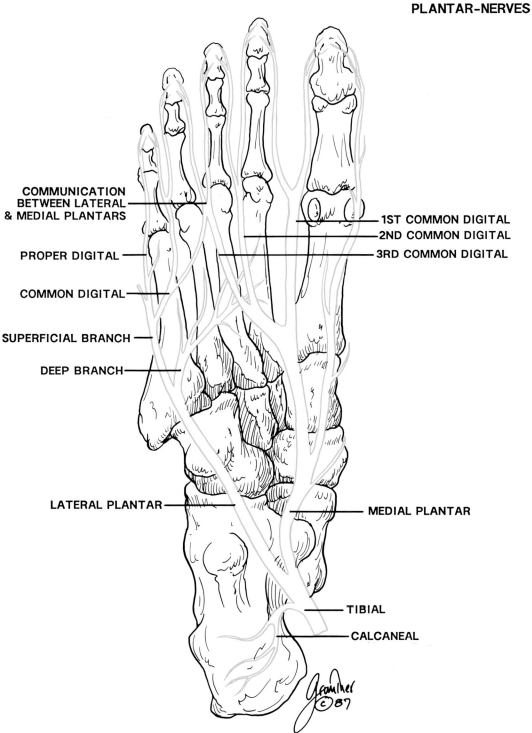

COMMUNICATION
BETWEEN LATERAL
& MEDIAL PLANTARS

1ST COMMON DIGITAL

2ND COMMON DIGITAL

PROPER DIGITAL

3RD COMMON DIGITAL

COMMON DIGITAL

SUPERFICIAL BRANCH

DEEP BRANCH

LATERAL PLANTAR

MEDIAL PLANTAR

TIBIAL

CALCANEAL